MW00973771

Volume 1

Practice Management from A to Z

A READABLE GUIDE TO A HEALTHY PRACTICE

Steve Cartin

Three Twenty-Three Publishing
Augusta, Georgia (USA)

Three Twenty-Three Publishing
315 Marshall St
Augusta, Georgia (USA) 30907
www.cartincoaching.com

Cover Design by Rachel Thomas & Melissa Whitley

Book Layout ©2013 BookDesignTemplates.com

Ordering Information:
Quantity sales. Special discounts are available on quantity purchases by corporations, associations, and others. For details, contact the "Special Sales Department" at the address above.

Practice Management from A to Z, Vol. 1/ Steve Cartin. —2nd ed.
ISBN-10: 1497396697 / ISBN-13: 978-1497396692

Dedicated to

The three men who have most impacted my life.

Vernon Miller taught me to write and encouraged me to read;

Furman Redd, taught me what was most important to read;

Art Balog taught me that seeing potential in people and showing them respect earns you the right to share what you've read.

Acknowledgements

Getting to this point from a distance once so far away can only happen with the help of gracious friends, insightful colleagues and patient loved ones. Writing a book about how to grow a healthy dental practice doesn't seem like the storyline for someone who had only seen the dentist twice before age twenty-two.

Cathy Sanders Erickson gave me the first bump in that direction by taking me on as a consultant to her start-up company, Dental Systems, Inc., back in the early 90s. The company had 71 clients (dentists) in the Houston, TX area. By 1995, I had decided that the consulting I did for Dental Systems could be done for dental practices also. But I had missed one key component of that equation: I had no dental office experience. Currently, I still provide consulting to Dental Systems, Inc. who now serve 2,000 dentists with their flagship product, *Insurance Answers Plus*. And so that began my dental career.

Providence brought a steady stream of helpers to one who needed more help than most. Like Cathy Erickson, there were others in the dental community who gave me opportunity: Linda Drevenstedt, Drs. John and Cathy (Ph.D.) Jameson and Dr. Stephen H. Dunn, DDS. Vicki Nashert provided my first formal training in practice management. She's a real pro; and without Vicki Sanco's expert help and guidance, Cartin Coaching & Management would have never caught air beneath its wings. There were clients who took a chance on me, fresh off of a couple years with Jameson Management and the great training it provided: Dr. Stephen H. Dunn, Dr. Philip Lewis, Dr. Paul McEvoy, Dr. Bobby Chokker and Dr. Lawrence Keegan. Event Coordinators gave me a platform: The Irish Dental Hygienists Association, Dr. Van Haywood, Dr. Kevin Frazier, Dr. Randy Sanders, Dr. Bill Williams and Ms. Lynn Thigpen. And there were those who fired me up – Ken Blanchard, Linda Miles, Tommy Moore and all my colleagues at *Lead Like Jesus*.

What seemed a chance meeting with Will Gunnels at the South Carolina Dental Association's Annual Meeting on April 26, 2008 inspired me that day to purchase a laptop as the first official action toward founding Cartin Coaching & Management. He introduced me to Dr. Van Haywood. Will Gunnels and Dr. Haywood are the roots from which two-thirds of my US-based speaking and consulting have grown.

My adult children – Rebekka, Rees and Rachel – and now my wife, Sandra, have endured the frequent travel, 30 trips of average 10 day length to the UK and Ireland, not to mention the speaking, consulting, coaching and prospecting throughout the Southeastern United States. Sandra encouraged me to begin writing several years ago. Rachel created the conceptual design for the book cover and has been my on-call graphic designer and bookkeeper. Rees is ever the marketing pump-me-up that I so often need and offers great marketing and business advice.

Some exceptionally resourceful people came into my pathway from seemingly nowhere – Mr. Will Parrish and Dr. Bill Davis – with whom I have collaborated to found Southeast Dental Advisors. They have become regular "go-to guys" in dental practice matters which go beyond the standard practice management coaching topics.

Last but certainly not least is Dr. Robert Loar, retired Navy dentist of 34 years, a close friend and fellow church member who has poured over and given keen marketing and business advice in addition to his dental and stylistic suggestions. He gives earthly validation to the prophetic Hebrew proverb, "[T]here is a friend who sticks closer than a brother (Proverbs 18.24)." Much of the passion and business thinking for this book evolved over numerous early morning breakfasts with the Good Doctor at the Evans Diner.

Practice Management from A to Z may well have failed for lack of the support and guidance of any one of these whom I have mentioned. Space does not permit the mention of all those who gave generously of their wisdom, support, promotion and counsel. Their individual and combined efforts are not annotated on the pages of this book but their imprint on me is lasting. For each one of you, I am grateful. Together, you helped me give myself a wonderful birthday gift as twenty-eight minutes ago I turned fifty-six years young. Thank you, one and all. I am truly grateful.

Steve Cartin
Augusta, Georgia
March 18, 2014

Foreword

All dentists want to have a successful practice with an empowered and accountable team of winners. Achieving that dream is not as easy as it looks. In dental school, dentists learn to do clinical dentistry with very little emphasis on practice and team development. It is not until they get out of dental school, highly in debt that they realize the tools for running a business and leading a team are very much a necessity...but where on earth can they find the crash course they need to start off on the right foot?

Other dentists have struggled with practice management and team development their entire career. How wonderful it would have been for them to have had a book like this to follow step by step early in their practices before they stepped on a few landmines. How handy it would have been before they fell into a deep hole of despair saying, "If I could just take care of my patients and do the dentistry without all this *other stuff.*" Other stuff includes hiring/training/trusting and empowering a group of employees. Then there is the overhead control, budgeting, technology, record keeping, case presentation, marketing and dozens of other things they feel ill prepared to do.

They can search the internet for bits and pieces. They can ask the more seasoned dentists how they do things. They can hire a management consultant or coach, or they can search for the book that covers these topics from A to Z.

There are good books on the market. Some cover systems of management, some cover philosophy of success, while others cover business principles that apply to dentistry. None cover as many topics as thoroughly as this readable guide to a healthy practice by Steve Cartin.

In reviewing this book, I am impressed by the thoroughness of the content. From Leadership to Risk Management (backups), to life balance and daily practice management essentials. These include confirming appointments, scheduling, telephone techniques, team meetings and financial arrangements. It's all there (From A to Z).

Employing the right staff is one of the toughest jobs as a dentist. Some hire in haste which makes waste. Others hire because they like the person they interviewed, which has nothing to do with their knowledge of dentistry or their work ethic. One of the most devastating things management consultants and coaches deal with in private practices is the long term employee that has never wanted to go the extra mile, never been excited about the success of the practice yet they remain on the team. Some people have jobs. Smart dentists want their employees to have careers. They want them to be self-motivated, caring and interested in the growth potential of the business. In the following chapters Steve outlines what to look for, how to train them and when it is time to let go if in fact they are not right for your practice.

This book is considered the "practice management bible!" This is a guide that you will refer back to many times over in the course of a year. In the easy to follow format of being alphabetized, you can quickly review the part that you are looking for. Do yourself a favor and keep it handy. Make notes in the margins; highlight the parts that apply most to your areas of weakness. Don't loan the book to a dentist friend....you may forget who has it. Instead, share a copy as a gift to your friends. If you're a study club organizer, invest in a copy for each of your study club members. Team and practice development is as easy as 1-2-3 – just follow the A, B, C's of this book.

Linda Miles
Practice Management Consultant/Speaker/Author
Founder, Linda Miles and Associates 1978
Founder, Speaking Consulting Network 1997
CoFounder, Oral Cancer Cause Foundation 2012
CoFounder, EPIC II 2014

Preface

How will you use this book? Why was it written?

You can't help but learn a few things about practice management in twenty years of serving the dental industry. Eight years working with scores of local practices underscores many of the same lessons again and again: it's often a series of smaller issues, rather than larger ones, which hinder a practice from reaching its full potential. Your dental practice offers broad and satisfying opportunity for business ownership, enough varying interests to keep you engaged: technology, patient care, business development, marketing, leadership, etc. Yet, the dental practice is not so large or complex that the owner cannot get a good grasp on all the systems and protocols which make for successful and satisfying practice ownership.

The chapters that unfold on the following pages come in various styles and with differing approaches. Some are step-by-step guides for accomplishing a task or scripts for conversations with patients or other team members. Others are more philosophical with proven principles around which you can refine your own current systems. Hopefully, each chapter will motivate you to some action or assessment.

You may choose to read this book straight through and assess your practice as you go along. You may scan the chapters and look for the best opportunities for jump-starting progress in a particular area of interest. The subheadings in the Table of Contents provide some insight into the contents of each chapter. Occasional references to other chapters point to further detail on specific subsystems but, generally, each chapter stands on its own.

The Endnotes provide an outstanding list of books which will add to your further development in life, business, leadership and dentistry.

Make sure to read the *Afterword*. Now would be a good time to do that; you know, the "read-the-back-of-the-book-to-see-how-it-ends" approach. The *Afterword* will give you added fuel for your journey to a happier, healthier practice.

Hope is not a strategy. Too often I've visited with dentists who hope tomorrow will be better. Or next month. Or next year. When the day, month or year has disappeared, the opportunity to have made it better has disappeared as well. The fact that you are reading this *Preface* gives the author hope, however – hope that you will go on to more productive, less stressful days where team members are fulfilled and patients are healthy. Read, review, plan and implement and your hope will be headed toward reality.

Contents

What reason, other than the fact that I want this

to work, do I have for believing that tomorrow

is going to be different from today?[1]

—Henry Cloud

CHAPTER 1

A – Automatic Data Backups

"Wisdom comes from experience.

Experience comes from mistakes."

T hat's what the sign at the church down the street said to me several years ago upon returning from a trip abroad. I'll never forget how its truth struck me. I thought back to the conversation on the ride between the airport and my first dinner meeting with a new client. I had arrived in his country to conduct an Initial Practice Assessment, much of which had been framed by the data I received in various practice management reports. Those reports were a keen reminder to my new client – and to me – of one of the key issues I cover in my first meeting with a client. The questions would be no different for any small business that wanted to guard against unexpected lost revenue. However, Dr. Franks' story on the drive to St. Andrews had told all that needed to be told.

Dr. Franks: *"Steve, you wouldn't believe how incredibly stressful the past month has been. The data package I sent you – it the last thing generated by my system before it crashed and took with it the last three years of patient and clinical data."*

I: *"What happened, Dr. Franks?"*

Dr. Franks: *"The lady at the front desk was new, and I thought it would be easiest if I asked my software vendor to produce the reports you requested. So while we were at lunch about a month ago, the vendor logged in remotely, produced the reports and emailed them to you. When we returned to the office, the system was down. We booted up and logged in. Nothing. No patient data whatsoever – it had been wiped out, every patient from A to Z, gone, and all the associated clinical and personal data was empty. Thankfully, we had printed a schedule for the day and had some idea who was coming in and for what. While trying to see them as best we could, the vendor was working furiously with Sarah at the front desk to see what had happened. Whatever they had done remotely caused a crash of our system. It was a Friday so we called my IT guy who agreed to meet me at the practice at 9 AM Saturday morning. He was able to calm my frayed nerves somewhat by reassuring me we could get the data from the secondary hard drive which was located in the closet. With things as bad as they were, I didn't want to risk doing it myself."*

Protocol

Question # 1: *Do you have automatic daily backups of your software?*

Your patient data is your life. Without overly exaggerating things, it could be your death. I first learned this lesson back in 2008 while serving as an Interim Practice Administrator in a large general restorative office in Florida. Our system died mid-morning one day and we were dead in the water. New hardware and software had recently been installed, and everyone was still somewhat unfamiliar with its function and use. We don't know what happened. But a quick call to our IT vendor in Atlanta, and they were on top of things. The corrupted data was scrubbed and removed. A couple of hours later we were back up and running. The restoration of system data from the backup was successful.

So we thought.

The backup had not been performed for several days. Somehow a power switch had been inadvertently knocked off and the battery backup had worked until it ran out of juice. Thankfully, the period between "juice" and "failure" was only a few days. We had Daysheets and were still documenting everything in paper charts because the team was still in training with electronic charting. It took some work but we were able to recreate the lost data from the paper charts. The radiographs were on a separate drive.

My international client was not so lucky. He picked up his story with the Saturday morning meeting between himself and his IT guy.

> *"When my IT technician was not able to access the backup drive from the terminal at the front desk, he immediately grew worried. The backup drive did not show up on the system. A quick visit to the closet revealed it was not operating.*
>
> *To make a long story short, my client's backup had died some time ago. The technician took it back to his office and phoned later to say that the drive had frozen up three years earlier. All hope of restoring data was not lost. Dr. Franks had data. He just didn't have any data from the last three years of patients he had seen. No chart notes. No indication of previous restorations versus those he had delivered. No probing records. No letters to specialists. Nothing."*

Location

Question # 2: *Where do you store the backed up information?*

Onsite is obviously a problem in the event of a fire or catastrophic event in your building. I remember the story of a local dentist who lost everything in a fire back in the early 2000s. It had prompted me to add these questions to my Initial Practice Assessment questionnaire. You can store your backup onsite but you run the risk of losing that backup in the event of a catastrophe such as this dentist had experienced. Storing them offsite or "in the cloud" is a safer, more reassuring plan, particularly if your backup service or system has a secondary drive in a separate geographical location. Redundancy comes with a price. When America sent men and women into space, redundant systems had to be in place to guarantee the safety of those on board. When you have a human on board, you not only need an oxygen system, you also need a backup to the oxygen system. And a backup to the backup. When it comes to your patient data, redundancy can be a life-saver for the practice. You don't need multiple redundancies but you do need a single redundant system. It will increase your protection exponentially.

Verification & Loss Protection

Question # 3: *When is the last time you tested your backed up data to ensure that your system is functioning properly?*

Depending on the system you have in place, you may be responsible for testing the backed system yourself. Make sure you're familiar with all steps you need to take in the event that data is lost and needs to be restored. If the backup system is located in your facility, make sure it is powered up.

Adding this one step to an end-of-day checklist can save you a lot of heartache, time and money down the road.

Your business insurance may cover business losses for equipment failures or extended power outages, but does it cover revenue losses due to data loss? Typically, this is an additional rider to your existing policy. Check with your insurance carrier to make sure you know the limits and possibilities of your policy.

Better safe than sorry.

As a result of Superstorm Sandy, 45 percent of small businesses in the Northeast were shut down by the storm – 20 percent of these were suffering this devastation due to data loss. Business Wire reports that subsequent to the storm, 40 percent of businesses put a new storm preparedness plan in place, another 16 percent [were] working on a plan, and more than 40 percent [had] chosen not to develop a new plan.[1]

During Hurricane Katrina when the author served as General Manager for Dental systems, Inc., a number of Southeast Texas dentists were temporarily out of business for storm-related issues, including lost data. Our own company quickly devised an emergency operations plan which included relocating all non-essential computing equipment upstairs in the event of flooding. Essential hardware and file storage systems were physically relocated further inland as a preventive measure for the possibility of more catastrophic damage. Hurricane scenarios typically provide enough warning to implement a plan. Fires, tornadoes, employee vandalism and other unexpected events make it prudent to have sufficient data preservation protocols even when you have no warning.

Up in the Air

The "cloud" offers two options for data protection. Your data can be backed up in the cloud through a number of existing service plans promoted online and at most state or regional annual meetings. It will be worth your while to speak to two or three vendors to verify that you are adequately protected and paying a reasonable fee for cloud storage. Even with data backed up online, periodically ensure that the cloud location is receiving the backups. You may have a dashboard application on your server or other computer that indicates the status of any particular backup. It may require a call to your service provider to determine the current status of your data. Train your team to never ignore any flag or error message relating to data backups. Occasionally, equipment fails to operate as planned and sometimes computer (digital) glitches force a shutdown of the backup process.

A second option for cloud backup exists for offices that use or desire cloud-based practice management software solutions. Aside from your terminals (small computing machines and keyboards), the processing and data storage all happen in the cloud. You may be in Missouri and your cloud may be in North Dakota. The "cloud" is actually on the *ground.* While these services and vendors typically have adequate redundancies, be sure you know what those redundancies are. Whether you're storing data in the cloud or using cloud-based software, ensure that the vendor/service you use is HIPAA-compliant.

For some offices, the availability of adequate internet bandwidth or dependability of internet connections makes a cloud-based practice management software less desirable or not feasible.

With proper planning and oversight you can all but eliminate revenue losses due to data loss. Nothing is foolproof. Waiting for a 100 percent perfect solution will be an effort in futility and is, of itself, the equivalent of putting it off or deciding against it.

Dr. Franks wished he had the opportunity to do all this again. He didn't.

You have the opportunity to get it right.

Now.

CHAPTER 2

B – Balance in Life

How many doctors create the practice of their dreams only to have home and family life sputter or even fall apart? How many have an excellent family life but wonder how they will support children in college and retirement because the practice has plateaued or is in decline? How many have a good home life and a better-than-average practice but find it harder and harder to enjoy either because of nagging, deteriorating health issues?

Golfers long to connect the ball with the club face at the exact location of the sweet spot. When they do --- pow! Writer Max Lucado argues for finding that sweet spot in life where everything seems to be firing on all cylinders. What could you do if you were impacting life with your sweet spot, that place where you were made to grow and thrive? Your business should serve your life; not the other way around. "Union University of Jackson, Tennessee requires all freshmen to evaluate their strengths. Students...string together pearls of success and celebration and wear the necklace.[1]" Knowing our strengths is important; recognizing and shoring up our weaknesses can spell the difference between a full or a frustrating life.

A Sweet Spot Parable

My first car was a 1970 Ford Custom 500, an aircraft carrier of sorts with a good ride and a low center of gravity, except when the tires were out of balance. When they were unbalanced, the faster I drove the more the car rattled and shook. The fix was simple: Find a service station that spin-balanced tires for about three dollars each. In the spin-balancing process, the technician attached a compass-like bubble level to the center of the tire. Then, electronically, he spun the tire at a very high rpm. As the tire spun, the bubble would move to a point corresponding to the highest centripetal force, where the weight of the tire was heaviest. The final step was using a rubber mallet to attach a small counter weight to the rim opposite the "heavy point". Voila! The tire was "balanced". Two points about spin-balancing tires teach us about imbalance in life: (1) The faster the speed or pace, the more discomfort is produced by the imbalance; and (2) Something must be "added" to the system in order to restore the balance and comfort.

Dentistry is a fast-paced business, complicated by the fact that the technician who is producing the lion's share of the revenue is generally too busy *producing* to spend time leading or managing. As a result, necessary chores which would be completed by managers of other businesses during the work day get moved over into *after-hours* time for the dentist. Any incursion into *after-hours* time reduces the focus and energy available for family, friends and much-needed personal pursuits and recreation. Dentists end up speeding down the highway of life with each increase in speed producing more imbalance.

Attempts to balance our out-of-balance lives often complicate the matter further. Internally, we have coping mechanisms which give off signals when life is out of balance. The natural response is to over compensate by doing more of what we feel good about and avoid those things we find difficult.

The result: Added imbalance.

Have you defined the areas of your life which need nurturing to discover your sweet spot, what Cartin Coaching calls *Sweetspot Dentistry*?

Cartin Coaching's Sweetspot Dentistry Assessment functions much like the "bubble compass" in our tire balancing illustration. Once diagnosed, it's up to the doctor to work on those areas, either alone or with the help of a qualified coach who can facilitate his or her progress. Through years of working with dentists in the U.S., U.K. and Ireland, we have identified four core areas of demand on the dentist and several specific sub areas within each core.

Professional

Every profession has its own blend of unique business demands. Dentistry is no different. You may be acquainted with the owner of the mid-sized auto repair shop where you take your car to be repaired. If you speak to him, you will find that some of the business demands are similar, some different. So what is it that makes dentistry professionally unique?

Clinical Dentistry & Hygiene

You have occasionally felt your friend's auto shop take a bite out of your wallet, but your friend at the auto repair shop doesn't have a clue about incisal surfaces, overjet or occlusion. Chet's work is technical. So is yours, but in a different field. For you, proficiency can easily mean a change in someone's quality of life, health and/or wellness. As your friend mastered his trade and business, he likely transitioned from lying beneath cars to sitting behind a counter or desk. Most dentists, however, will always be chairside six to eight hours a day. There are days you enjoy being a dentist. Other days, you wonder why you didn't become a banker, an attorney or an engineer. The demands on your time as a dental practice owner are unique. As you get more and more proficient in your technical work, you remain chairside rather than climbing the ladder to a corner office with a view.

There are some procedures you enjoy doing more than others. There are some with which you feel your skills are more advanced than with others. You have either developed a great unspoken rapport with your assistant, are struggling with it or growing in those team skills. And you work to improve your systems for checking hygiene as the demands for operative dentistry grows. Your level of comfort with clinical dentistry and hygiene is but one area of your life that figures into the equation to determine your dental sweet spot.

Business and Administrative

Here's where you can relate to Chet. Each month bills and employees must be paid. Each month you email your data to the accountant and receive a monthly report of your profit and loss. Each day the Daysheet gives you a pretty good summary of how business was that day. You may even drop the deposit off at the bank. Daily, monthly and annually you keep a close eye on the budget, knowing that any deviation from it will result in a change to your take home pay – good or not so good. The kicker is that Chet gets to work on these things a little along every day, between customer or staff needs. You don't have that luxury. Tending to the business matters of a dental office can be very taxing on dentists who don't have appropriately trained staff, good systems and select vendors/services in place to ease the burden. The more productive the practice becomes, the more stress it places on the system.

Cartin Coaching finds that many doctors are unduly burdened by inefficient business and administrative systems in the practice. As you add these concerns to those you have about clinical dentistry and hygiene, stress begins to mount. Yet, we're only one-sixth of the way through the topics contained in the *Sweetspot Dentistry Assessment.*

Patients, PR & Marketing

You calm the anxious, caution the impetuous, cater to the demanding and place care calls to the hurting. Dentistry is a people business. Dentists aren't the only face of the practice, but the demand for the dentist to be a people person and a student of people's healthcare and consumer behaviors can be overwhelming. Everything you do is marketing – the way you give an injection, your chairside manner and your relationship with your staff. Women and men who don't master the people side of dentistry either naturally or by hard work struggle to stay ahead of the game, all other things being equal. Refining your clinical protocols, putting the best face on the practice and communicating your excellence to the community require hard work. Some dentists are more suited to it than others. Finding your sweet spot in dentistry doesn't demand that you become "the" expert in all these areas; but you must assure someone – staff or vendor – is minding the store in a proactive manner.

Most dentists give considerable attention to these unique areas of their sweet spot. They must. Yet, doing so to the neglect of other areas can cause the "tire of life" to be overly weighted in one of four quadrants. Three quadrants remain.

Family

For purposes of our discussion, we define family as both immediate and extended. It includes those who live in the same house and those who have matured and taken up homes of their own. Our society has aged considerably over my adult life. According to the U.S. Government's Administration on Aging, the number of Americans who are sixty-five years of age or older will almost double between 2009 and 2030.[4] Americans who reached age 65 in 2009 are projected to live another 19.2 years, a full 5 years longer than in 1960. The number of adults 55 years of age who have significant responsibilities taking care of aging parents has increased significantly and continues the climb.[5] These demographic factors along with cultural and societal changes demand more and more of dentists today in regard to family life than at any time in the history of oral healthcare.

Leadership

Leadership comes to mind as a "professional" pursuit. So why not include it under the *professional* category? According to management expert, Ken Blanchard, the definition of leadership spans various areas and pursuits in our lives. Blanchard says,

> *"Any time you seek to influence the thinking, behavior or development of another person, you take on the role of a leader."*

Leadership is about going somewhere. We give ready assent to that definition of leadership in the workplace. It also applies at home, with friends and in the community. People have varying levels of desire for influencing others to action, thought or growth. It would be a rare person indeed who had none of those desires. Three unique spheres of leadership play out in the lives of dentists.

When English Poet John Donne penned the words, "No man is an island," he could have been thinking of dentists like you. The author stopped in to interview the town dentist in San Marcos de Colon, Honduras. It was surprising to find the dentist working alone in the office. This happens in U.S. dentistry on those rare occasions when the dentist meets a patient at the practice on an emergency call. The successful practice of dentistry requires the coordinated work of a team. Challenging team members with varied skills, different levels of experience and unique personalities requires the best of leadership efforts. The dentist leads team members one-on-one and in the relationships of functional work units: the business team, the clinical team, etc. He or she must also lead the entire team in order to guide the practice to its desired goals. Achieving the desired level and outcomes of leadership require discipline and commitment. Even when dentists get it right at the office, they close the door behind them at the end of the day to head home to a different set of leadership challenges.

Home Life

Most dentists go home each day to a spouse and/or children. Some dentists have the added stress of parenting children alone. Leadership issues extend beyond the dental practice to those in our immediate family. The goals may be different but the essential elements of motivating, coordinating, guiding and serving are just as intact at home as in the dental practice. The dentist may not lead with the same style at home, and that creates additional leadership demands on the dentist.

If you have children, the fact that they may be adults does not remove the home-based leadership challenges you face. But children and a spouse at home require and deserve our very best. Are you more successful in leadership at home than at the office or vice versa? Why? What dynamics can you identify that help you understand better how you may need to modify your leadership style once you leave the office?

Families need more than leadership. They need nurture, support and guidance. Some would argue (and rightfully so, the author judges) that these are all bundled up within leadership. Whether you see them as integral within *or* complementary to leadership, none of them can be ignored by the dentist who desires a healthy, happy home life.

Extended Family & Friends

Do you have an aging parent or parents? Is there a nephew or niece who looks up to you as a role model? The role you're modeling may be as a business person, healthcare provider, father or caretaker. It could be the role of a spiritual leader. Your leadership role with extended family and friends will not be as clearly defined as in the dental practice. While these roles may not be as consistently called upon in home life, the leadership challenges are real. They summon our very best because we know it matters.

Again, time plays a factor in your ability to discharge all the leadership demands upon you. Do you work a five-day week? Or do you work four days? Do you leave for the day before others in the home wake up? What time do you arrive back home? How much time is left over after the office and occasional weekend continuing education courses to invest in the lives of those you care about outside your immediate home?

Back in the mid-80s, I was burning the candle at both ends with forty plus hours a week as an flight test project manager in the Air Force, significant non-profit commitments in the community, a wife and two young children. I turned to a wise, fatherly-figure mentor for advice about what I could give up of my commitments in the community. After working through them one-by-one, I could not identify a single commitment I wanted to relinquish. Not dissuaded about the reality that something had to change, I mapped out a typical week on two large pieces of graph paper taped together (pre-spreadsheet days). I divided each of my waking hours into fifteen-minute segments. What I discovered was not that I didn't have enough time but that I had my time spaced out such that there were inefficient gaps everywhere. I focused my attention on tightening up my schedule and moving my sleep hours to retire earlier and, thus, rise earlier. In just a few weeks there was new wind in my sails. Just as inefficient gaps in your operative schedule can make you unproductive at the office, the format and design of your schedule away from the office has an impact on your ability to live out your leadership roles among extended family and friends.

Summary & Moving Forward

As a dental professional you must balance clinical concerns, business matters and the myriad relationships with patients, staff members, and vendors. You provide leadership to individuals, small teams and the entire staff in the office each day. And when you clock out at the end of the day, you must either exercise leadership at home or default on that responsibility. If it's a Friday afternoon, you know that the weekend ushers in a new set of challenges with extended family and close friends. Will you spend your Saturday at another continuing education course or fly home to Maryland to check on your beloved mother who just recently said goodbye to your Father? Will there be time to get enrolled at the local gym so you can start working on your weight and on decreasing your blood pressure? What will you do for the mental or spiritual growth that does not cry out daily but hits a brick wall when left unattended? It's no wonder dentists find it difficult to create balance in their lives.

It is beyond the scope of this survey of essential practice management concepts to fully define the other six areas. But you will recognize the challenge they bring. In addition to *professional* demands and *leadership* demands, the dentist – like everyone else in life -- will find whole life balance only when *emotional* and *physical* demands are appropriately nurtured.

You may want to inquire further about the *Sweetspot Dentistry Assessment* to help you identify areas you need to develop further in your own life. Like the earlier example of spin-balancing tires, a good assessment can help you determine where "weight" needs to be added in order to counterbalance the rough spots on the four wheels of your life –

professional, family, emotional and physical. Your ride may be shaky because one wheel is out of balance. In addition to the six specific areas already discussed, you will also want to consider the following areas of Emotional and Physical balance:

- Financial Independence
- Personal development
- Renewal & Relaxation
- Physical Conditioning & Health
- Spiritual Development
- Significance & Legacy

Some books such as Strength Finders[6] advise to work toward areas of strength in life. When going for balance, however, the task is not about talents alone. Personal health is not about fat, carbohydrates and protein alone. It is also about exercise, vitamins, minerals, antioxidants and much more. So also, the strength you have for *living the abundant life* is multifaceted. All of the essential elements of life must be appropriately nurtured if one is to find balance in life.

Which area needs most work right now in your life? Clinical Dentistry & Hygiene? Family? Social, Intellectual & Emotional? Physical Conditioning & Health?

Where do you need to start?

CHAPTER 3

C – Confirming Appointments

Practice management techniques have come a long way in the past thirty years. One area which has seen many advances is that of confirming appointments. In 1985, there were two primary means for confirming a patient's appointment: the telephone and postcards. Today, we have added automatic telephone notification (and response systems), text messages and emails. Call me a purist, but I still believe nothing serves better than voice-to-voice communication unless the patient has specifically opted for another form of notification. Opinions will vary on this from consultant to consultant. There are some outstanding automated systems out there today for aiding in the confirmation process. But one fact remains:

A confirmation is not a confirmation
until you receive a response from the patient.

Until you do, your attempt has only been a reminder, assuming they received that attempt.

Let's pose some questions to help you think through the effectiveness of the confirmation systems in your practice. As you consider these questions, you will find that telephone confirmation becomes so much easier when you adhere to a few basic principles.

Which patients do you need to confirm?

None of them. The question, as posed, is a trick question. You don't confirm patients, you confirm appointments. Understanding this and being able to communicate it to the patients you serve will go a long way toward helping you maintain an attitude of vigilance over the daily schedule. It will help you in tactfully responding to those who bristle at the suggestion that they might not show up for their appointment. So, let's re-word the question: Which *appointments* do you need to confirm?

If you have been in your current practice for a year or more, you already know a great number of patients who do not need their appointments confirmed. These are the patients who keep their appointments like clockwork. A good verbal skill to use with them would be:

> *"Susan, you're one of our best patients; if everyone was as responsible with their appointments as you are, it surely would make my job*

easier. How would you like for me to confirm your next appointment or would you prefer that I do not?

The first principle is this: Prioritize your confirmation calls according to a patient's history of keeping their appointments.

Some patients do not have much history with your practice. So always confirm new patients until either: a) they have a history of keeping their appointments or, b) they specifically request not to be called, confirmed or otherwise reminded.

When do you confirm?

The exact answer to this question varies from practice to practice. Three other questions need to be asked first:

Question 1: How long is your quick call list, the list of patients who have committed to a procedure or appointment but who currently do not have a next appointment for that procedure?

Question 2: How full is your hygiene schedule for the next week or your operative schedule for the next two weeks?

Question 3: Have you identified patients on your current schedule who would be happy to take an earlier appointment?

If you have a long list of patients waiting to see the hygienist or dentist and your hygiene and operative schedule is substantially full, you might wait until one to two days prior to confirm appointments. On the other hand, a short list of patients waiting to be treated or a gappy appointment book on either side (operative or hygiene) may require you to confirm three or four days in advance, even a week. Experience indicates that telephone confirmation more than a week out is spottily effective at best.

Another factor which needs to be considered in answer to the question "when to confirm" is lab work. Most practices I've worked in have experienced frustration on occasion because they confirmed appointments before the lab work was back in the practice. Are any of the following experiences familiar in your practice?

Bad Experience of the 1st Degree: The patient shows up but the lab work has not. It's difficult to explain to a patient why you went to the effort to ask him to confirm his lunchtime appointment when you must meet him at the front desk with, "I'm sorry, we have not received your crown from the lab."

Bad Experience of the 2nd Degree: You realize in the morning meeting that the lab case for Mrs. Gruffy has not shown up. So the doctor and office manager jump through hoops to put the squeeze on the lab to rush it over before her noon appointment. Mrs. Gruffy doesn't know the difference, but a lot of energy that could have been used for improving the practice was spent just keeping it afloat for the next few hours.

What if you can't confirm?

Here is a scheduler's nightmare: a hygiene schedule with three blocks which haven't been confirmed, one at 9 a.m., another at 11:30 a.m. and a third one at 4 p.m. What's more, each of these three patients has missed an appointment in the last three years, all with "shaky" excuses. Do you double book? Do you cancel the original appointment and try to book another patient into the slot? How do you keep your patients happy and engaged with the practice? How do you keep the doctor and hygienist happy about today's schedule?

You are not going to solve this one all at once. Be thankful that you're not chasing down lab cases for patients later in the day. Even so, it is not going to be the best day in the practice. The morning meeting ends at 7:58 a.m. and it's time to get started.

Let's take a two-pronged approach with the assumption that you've been diligent to collect the cell phone numbers of each of the patients in question. If you haven't, the solution below might work but the likelihood isn't as great. Commit to getting as many cell phone numbers as you can for a rainy day. It will pay off.

Step 1: Ask the hygienist to take a look at the quick call list and suggest several options for patients who won't need the entire hour. Simultaneously, leave a message for the 9 a.m. patient who has not yet confirmed. You might say,

> *"Suzy, this is Cheri at Dr. Jones' office. We are concerned that you may not have received our confirmation request for your 9 o'clock hygiene appointment or that something has come up. We hope you're okay. Please let us hear from you by 8:30 or we will need to move a waiting hygiene patient into that slot."*

Step 2: Call the 11:30 a.m. and 4:00 p.m. patients with a similar message, giving them a deadline for confirming that is an hour and a half before their appointment.

Step 3: If Suzy hasn't confirmed by 8:30 a.m., fill the 9:00 a.m. appointment if possible with a patient who won't need the full hour in the hygienist's chair. Notify that patient that if he or she can be at the office between 9 and 9:15 a.m., the hygienist will be able to complete the appointment even if it runs a few minutes past 10 a.m. You know it won't run that long, but the patient doesn't know. In fact, unless the 10:00 a.m. patient is Mrs. Gruffy's husband, the hygienist might be happy to let the appointment run until 10:05 a.m. and make up the five minutes in the next appointment or later in the day. It's less likely that a patient will feel like a "plug" in a hole if he or she isn't checking out right at 10 o'clock. Make sure you phone Suzy to let her know that her slot is no longer available. Be cheerful. Let her know that you understand. The less she feels like she let you down, the more likely she will be to re-engage for a new appointment.

> *"Suzy, I'm sorry that we needed to put a waiting patient into the 9 o'clock appointment you were not able to confirm. I didn't want you to be subject to the $50 cancellation fee so I did what I thought was best for you and for Suzanne (the hygienist). I hope this decision works out well for you and that nothing bad has happened that got in your way. We look forward to hearing from you really soon so we can get you back into your scheduled care."*

Step 4: Do your best to fill the 11:30 a.m. and 4 o'clock appointments in the same manner, only now you will have 90 minutes advance notice to fill each of the slots. Will this approach work every time? Absolutely not. Will it work much of the time? Yes. So…

What to do with time you can't "quick fill"?

If the hygienist is on salary, then the doctor isn't going to be particularly happy. If she is on commission, the hygienist isn't going to be particularly happy. But she will be happier than she would have been if the appointment was double booked and both patients arrived for the same appointment. Double booking has the potential to upset the patient, upset the hygienist, upset the reception team and upset the doctor. Why would you want to run that risk? Idle time in the hygiene chair should not become idle time for the hygienist. Hygienists should be part of the team just like everyone else, and their employment agreements should reflect the expectation to help fill the schedule, when needed, or work on other short projects.

There should always be growth projects in the practice, things to do that build up the practice when those scarce spare minutes allow time to focus on other things. Avoid filling the hygienist's time with "busy" work. But if no suitable project presents itself as an opportunity, there are a number of things a hygienist can do to increase her contribution to the team:

- Confirm the hygiene schedule for the next day or two. It will be good for her to have this extra connection with her patients.
- Sign and address birthday or anniversary cards to patients.
- Review charts in depth for the following day to see what opportunities exist for referring operative treatment to the doctor.

- Etc.

Some of these things would normally be the responsibility of other members of the practice. A day that falls apart is an opportunity for a team to come together. It's time to shed the "not my job" attitude and do whatever is possible to improve the day or reduce the stress other team members are dealing with.

What to do for a no-show?

You only have ten minutes to be concerned without sounding perturbed or desperate. If Suzy is expected and does not arrive within ten minutes of her appointed time, phone her immediately. You may get to speak with the patient but, chances are, you won't. In either case, your message should convey care, not frustration:

> *"Suzy, we hope you're okay. You don't normally miss your appointments. We were concerned that something urgent may have kept you from being here. Will you please call and let us know you're okay?"*

Don't tell Suzy that you want to get her back into the schedule when she returns your call. That sounds too much like a bait and switch. Suzy is an adult. She knows you want to get her back on the schedule. Further, you don't know what prevented her from attending or whether something life-changing has happened. When she does call, make sure you follow up on your concern for her. Make rescheduling a part of the call but not the main focus.

The longer you wait to make this call, the more it sounds like Suzy was an afterthought or that you are attempting either to solve your problem (the schedule) or to make her feel guilty. Ten minutes is long enough to wait; then call. Patients who slip through the cracks require five to ten times more effort to get back into the schedule than those who are followed up with immediately and courteously.

Summary

Adequately addressing all the issues around schedule confirmation is outside the scope of this present work. But tending to the issues above in an appropriate manner will help your practice be healthier and happier. The questions above are real world situations in a dental office. More than that, these are common situations. While many of the technology-based reminder systems are good and effective in their own right, it's easy to see why they are not the end-all answer to keeping your schedule full. Will your savvy new ITConfirm software be able to sort out whether Mrs. Gruffy's lab work is onsite before confirming her appointment? Probably not. Is it sophisticated enough to work through a hygiene schedule that fell apart between the moment you unlocked the door and when you started answering the phones? Not hardly.

The best defense against missed appointments is being on the offense confirming appointments without being offensive. Missed appointments will happen. When they do, resolve them with your best effort. Missed appointments are human problems, not technological ones. They need a human touch. Don't overlook the importance of the telephone for confirming appointments.

CHAPTER 4

D – Dental Assistants

A well-trained dental assistant provides one of your best opportunities to increase production while decreasing your own workload and stress. Doctors who have invested themselves into the professional development of their assistants are some of the happiest dentists in practice today. These doctors request the services of a practice management consultant with less frequency than those with less-skilled assistants. But this observation has little to do with whether the assistant has been certified or is on a registered list of qualified dental assistants. Seasoned dental consultants shouldn't get caught off guard by bad blood between a dentist and an assistant. But in my early days, this was not always the case. Since that first uncomfortable conversation, the few others which have followed have gone more like this:

Dr. Franks: *"Steve, I need you to help me do something about my assistant. She's got to go."*

Steve: *"Why?"*

Dr. Franks: *"Almost every day, or at least weekly, she makes the same mistakes. It drives me crazy. She doesn't set up the room correctly. She's doesn't give any attention to detail when she's packing cord. Her impressions are sloppy. She slumps in her chair and doesn't pay attention when she's suctioning a patient. The list goes on and on."*

Steve: *"Have you shown her how you want her to do those things?"*

Dr. Franks: *"She KNOWS how to do them; she's been assisting for twenty years!"*

Steve: *"Have you shown her how YOU want it done?"*

That's the point where Dr. Franks gets a look on his face that makes me wonder if he's going to fire his consultant before the consultation even gets started.

Training Assistants

Requirements for training and opportunities for expanded duties differ from state to state and from country to country. Even when a dental assistant is fully-qualified in all that her governing body will allow, that doesn't mean she will be the assistant the doctor needs or is pleased with. Just as every assistant is different, so is every doctor.

First, your assistant needs a comprehensive job description. In Cartin Coaching's Practice Management Systems, this comprehensive list of duties becomes the training checklist, and each duty is trained (explained and demonstrated) and documented by the trainer (yourself, Lead Assistant, Clinical Coordinator, etc). The documentation requires initials and a date by both the trainer and the trainee. It doesn't stop there.

The Assistant initials and dates each item after she has demonstrated the skill to the Trainer and after she has performed the skill successfully one or two times. At this point, both the Trainer and the Assistant have certified that the skill has been learned and demonstrated. (NOTE: This process is described in detail in Chapter 10: J - Job Performance).

Skills sometimes regress. Not to worry. We all fall short of one hundred percent now and then. When a skill has regressed to the point that it becomes a problem (*ie.,* it doesn't quickly correct itself), then "retrain" the skill and use the Training Form to indicate that retraining has taken place. The sooner you retrain the skill that has degraded, the easier it is to correct. Team members who are retrained later rather than sooner create additional frustration with each appointment or patient they do not serve properly. Not only will this retraining reinforce to the dental assistant that there has been some slip up in job performance, it provides a documented account of that regression, attested to by both the assistant and the trainer. Training dental assistants doesn't need to keep you awake at night. You need a system and you need to work the system. If you have more than one assistant, you will want to personally ensure that the most qualified assistant is fully-versed in how you want each item trained. For that Lead Assistant, at least one more duty is added to the list of her job responsibilities:

> *Train all assistants using the office Training Documentation Form.*

Expanded Duties

One sure method for increasing production in a dental practice is to delegate all the duties which you can legally and ethically delegate to the lowest paid level on your team. One doctor I worked with in a large clinic which specialized in dentures and implants had this delegation down to a science. Each step of the process – from initial consult to final delivery of dentures – was delegated to a dental assistant or to a lab technician (which he had onsite), freeing his time to do what he alone was authorized to do. Imagine how unproductive you would be if you had to take all the radiographs in your practice. It is hard to imagine a practice that operates this way today. But it is no different when a doctor insists on taking impressions, packing cord, or recementing a temporary when the governing body permits it to be done by an assistant.

You may want to check with your state's dental association to get the latest information on what can and can't be delegated. This call will pay dividends many times over if you discover only one part of a procedure which you can begin to delegate. Make a list of things you can delegate that you are not consistently delegating at this time:

You can hardly make a better investment in your practice than that of sending an assistant to a course to gain proficiency in an expanded duty. When she completes the course and returns to the office, immediately have her trained in *your* way of doing it. Dr. Gary DeWood, formerly of the Pankey Institute, says,

> *"Build careers for your team, don't just give them a job. Team members who have the ability to focus on the future inspire confidence in your patients. People who just have a job rarely have this ability. Invest in them!*[1]

Auxiliary Ears

Once you have made a recommendation to a patient or completed a restoration or other treatment, make sure to use your assistant's ears as auxiliaries to your own.

When assessing patient flow and care in a practice, I sometimes notice that at the end of the procedure or exam, the doctor is busy with a chart or other matter in the operatory while the assistant escorts the patient to check out. Don't do that!

Instead, learn to coordinate with your assistant so that you have the benefit of her ears listening to the patient when you are out of the room. Patients routinely ask questions of assistants that they do not want to ask the doctor. When you prevent that opportunity of exchange from taking place, you lose an important advantage in your efforts to deliver the best possible care to your patients. Make sure your assistants have alone time with patients *before* and *after* your time with them. Assistants can be a valuable resource for affirming your recommendations, allaying patient fears or simply helping the patient understand things he or she was not comfortable getting clarity from with you. If you're Sherlock Holmes, your assistant is Dr. Watson.

Strive to be the best two-person team in all of dentistry.

Charts

Few things restrict an assistant's ability to serve you and the practice well like being ill-equipped to handle patient charts. Let's talk about before *and* after the appointment.

At the beginning of the day – or at the end of the previous day – your assistant should review the charts of everyone whom you will see that day. Later (Chapter 13: M – Morning Meetings), we will cover this in more detail. For now, remember that in your patients' charts are clues and signposts which point to greater financial success in the practice – needed treatment, overdue hygiene, past due accounts, etc. Before the day begins, your assistant should be thoroughly familiar with the patients you will see and with the needs of each of those patients.

Let's take a moment to address treatment room set up in connection with our discussion of charts. Before the patient is escorted from the reception lounge, the patient's chart should already be displayed on the computer screen in the operatory. Not being fully prepared for the patient who has been escorted to the treatment room presents an unprofessional image. Here's a *Do-and-Don't* example which demonstrates the importance of your dental assistant being familiar with patient charts:

DON'T say,

"Good morning, Mrs. Smith. What are we going to do today?"

DO say,

"Good morning, Mrs. Smith. I know you're happy that we're going to take care of the sensitivity you've been having on your lower left side today."

Which statement would make you feel better as a patient? The DON'T statement suggests we have not prepared to see the patient. The DO statement confirms that we know exactly what Mrs. Smith's appointment is about today. She will have a better experience because the dental assistant has taken the effort to be fully prepared for the appointment.

When the patient has left the operatory or office, the assistant needs to be fully capable and prepared to complete the chart notes which the doctor will sign off after his or her review. You may have certain templated notes set up in your practice management software to aid in this process. Be careful not to template quantities or measurements such as how much anesthetic was delivered or how deep the canal was drilled so as not to inadvertently have the wrong information entered into the patient's chart. An assistant who can complete chart notes according to the doctor's standard contributes to a less stressful day. One who consistently has to ask about routine matters or who enters chart notes inattentively is like a dripping faucet that you can't turn off. Get this right and your days will go much more smoothly.

CHAPTER 5

E – Employing Staff

"Train a good staff member and you can't keep 'em;
get a bad one and you can't get rid of 'em."
—Anonymous

Hiring staff can bring great pleasure or produce great pain. But surely the above quote is not correct. Surely you can keep a good staff member. And you can easily dismiss a bad staff member, can't you? The answer might not be as easy as you expect. While most states are "right to work" states in regard to employment law, terminating a staff member brings many more considerations to the table in addition to those laws. Some questions which will arise are:

- *How* will we replace this staff member?
- *When* will we replace this staff member?
- How much will it *cost* to replace this staff member?

- Have we *exercised due diligence* to ensure this staff member's success?
- What impact will *another change* in staff have on the practice?
- Can we *update the job description* prior to making the new hire?
- What will we do *in the interim* before a new hire is identified?
- What guarantees that we will *do a better job of hiring* next time?
- What will this do to *my unemployment insurance rate*?
- Do I have all my *ducks in a row*?

Dismissing a staff member in any business is more complicated than one might imagine. Doing so in a busy dental office where the owner is tied up with his or her hands in someone's mouth for seven hours a day takes hiring and firing to a different, more complex level.

Costly Changes

Nailing down an exact number is impossible. However, expert guidance tells us the cost of hiring is more than we might guess. Consider the range of possibilities in two opinions from respected sources.

Writing in *Powerful Practice, Vol. 1,* Julie Weir states,

"Research has shown that replacing an employee costs a business a minimum of 1.5 times the employee's annual salary. These costs include the lost productivity due to the absence of the employee and the lost productivity of the doctor and other team members who are involved in the interviewing and training process of the employee's replacement. If a doctor has two employees turn over in a year, these costs could be between $75,000 [and] $180,000 to the practice, not to mention the stress of repeating this process on top of an already busy work schedule."[1]

In the present author's experience, Ms. Weir's estimate bounds the high end. In an article exploring the options for formal and informal background checks on prospective employees, The Small Business Administration cites a report from AARP which estimates that "...replacing an experienced worker *of any age* can cost 50 percent or more of the individual's annual salary in turnover-related costs, with increased costs for jobs requiring specialized skills, advanced training or extensive experience..."[2] Even at just 50 percent, the cost is significant. As a business owner, the cost comes out of your take-home pay. More reason to get it right.

The best way to avoid the cost and headaches associated with firing is to put the necessary elbow grease into hiring. Give close attention to the following five keys for hiring and your long-term success in business will begin a steady upward climb.

Dr. Henry Cloud, leadership coach to executives and CEOs offers some pointed advice for making a decision about keeping or not keeping an employee: "Take the past performance of the person…and project it into the future:

- Do I want this same level of performance a year from now?
- Do I want to be having these same conversations two years from now?

If the answer to these is no, then it is time to ask some other questions that get you to the real anatomy of hope:

- What reason is there to have hope that tomorrow is going to be different?
- What in the picture is changing that I can believe in?

…Endings are necessary when there is no hope."[3]

Once you have satisfied yourself that a new hire must be made, follow the five keys below to make the best hire you can for your practice, patients and team.

Recruit before Hiring

Many employers omit the vital role recruiting plays in the hiring process. Recruiting should be an ongoing effort in your practice. Keep in mind that just as everything you do is marketing, everything you do is recruiting. This is true because of all the people who see or hear your outdoor advertising, your monthly mailers, your radio ads, etc., some of these people are dental professionals. They are making an appraisal of what kind of practice you run by what they see and hear. Not only should your public face be geared toward patients, it should also attract the best and brightest dental staff to your brand.

Hosting a continuing education event or putting on a hands-on clinic is an excellent way to showcase areas of your particular expertise. While showcasing your brand, you also have the opportunity to informally meet potential team members who are motivated enough to attend training events. Make sure to keep contact details for future events. You can also use them when promoting a position you need to fill.

Another good opportunity for the recruiting process in a dental office is for the dentist and/or office manager to participate in dental events or charitable dentistry projects in your area. Doing so will give you another informal opportunity to observe team members in action whom you would otherwise know nothing about.

Some of the best reception and business team members may currently be in positions outside the dental industry. The waiting list for jobs as bell-hops, concierges and receptionists at upscale hotels is typically long for a reason. But getting on that list is a great first step. Routinely, the business men and women who pass through these hotels are impressed with the outstanding customer service rendered by such employees. It is a fairly common practice for those employees to be offered better paid positions outside the hotel.

You may not spend a lot of time in luxury hotels but you do business in customer-service oriented businesses every day. Make sure to always have business cards with you and don't be shy about sharing them when someone wows you with exceptional customer service. Likewise, banks have become training centers for "upselling". Customers who have checking accounts are encouraged to open savings accounts. Customers with frequent overdrafts are offered services to link accounts together in order to avoid those "one time" charges. Of course, the ongoing charge more than makes up for it, but the bank teller has been instructed to upsell the customer in as many ways as possible. Recognizing that this is *their job*, you might notice that a young man or woman is very courteously *doing* that job and doing it well. If you have a business card with you when others impress you with customer service or upselling skills, hand the person a card and say,

> *"May I share this business card with you? We do not currently have any positions available; but when we do, I would like to have your resume' on file. Would you be so kind as to send one that I can have for reference at a later time?"*

Not only will you begin to increase your ready stock of quality applicants, you will also make that person's day! Chances are, he or she will be encouraged to develop their customer service skills even more. Even if *you* never hire them, you've nonetheless invested in someone who believes quality makes a difference. That's a good thing.

Don't overlook supervised on-the-job training or temporary staff as excellent recruiting pools for future needs. Offering externships or internships gives you an opportunity to evaluate potential staff members without making a commitment. Offering "mock interviews" to recent graduates of dental training programs or technical schools might just turn up an outstanding candidate you would have never met otherwise. The majority of those who would come through such interviews in your office would receive the benefit of the interview experience only. One special candidate might find a career; and you might find an outstanding employee.

In short, recruiting is about attracting the right candidates, candidates who have an interest in your dental office and the kind of dentistry you do. Hiring is about selecting the best and brightest from among those qualified candidates.

Evaluate Your Need to Hire

Most dental offices run on minimum staffing in response to the slimmer profit margins in today's world. But you may have options other than hiring. As you assess whether you need a new hire, take into account the following factors:

- Any availability within your current team to absorb the unassigned duties without undue stress
- The skills of your current team
- Any cross-trained capabilities on your current team
- Appropriate vendors who may be efficiently secured to complete various business processes
- The place you're at in your annual work flow cycle (summer, holiday, etc)
- Any part-time employees who may be ready for full time employment

It will cost you significant money to make a new hire. Invest the money to do so only when you have convinced yourself that hiring another person is the most efficient, most sensible option.

Process, not Urgency or Bias

One of the easiest traps to fall into in the dental office is making a hiring decision on urgency or emotion. Select by process, not by urgency or bias. When you are down by one dental assistant, the days are long and hard. A potential candidate shows up at the office for an interview saying great things about your facility and looking her best. Remember, there is a reason she is looking for a job. Perhaps it is a very good reason. On the other hand, she may be unemployed for reasons that are not good. Or she may be employed but suspecting that the shoe is about to fall at any moment. People who turn up for a job interview want to get hired. Of course, they will say all the right things. However, all this does not necessarily add up to a hiring decision. Prospective employees are looking for a job and will stretch the truth, if not bend or break it, in order to become employed. Hiring a new employee, however, doesn't guarantee an added contribution to shouldering the workload in the practice.

Cartin Coaching has a hiring process that consists of several definitive steps aimed at helping you achieve a more unbiased selection and filter out bad apples. You may create your own process. Some elements to include are:

- Appropriately announcing and advertising the position
- Informal telephone screening of all candidates according to select criteria
- Selection of three best candidates from the telephone screening
- Layered interviews which score each candidate according to the same criteria
- Identifying the best candidate who meets all essential criteria and promises to be a good fit with other team members
- Making a written offer

Does it sound like a lot of work? It is. At least it's more work than the average office puts into a hiring decision. However, the best method for avoiding troubling firing decisions is making the best hiring decisions.

Trading Places

Occasionally, employers fall into the trap of trying to convince the potential candidate that this is the best office for them or a wonderful place to work. In essence, the employer trades places with the candidate and "seeks" his or her approval and willingness to join the team. If you find yourself in this situation, it's time to go back to the drawing board with recruitment to find candidates suited for your office. Neither should you oversell the practice to the potential candidate. An employee with an unmet expectation concerning his or her workplace, responsibilities or supervisor creates just as bad a situation as does an employer having unmet expectations in the employee. When a candidate gets excited about a potential job, it's common for the person to sidestep questions, the answers to which might be hard to accept. Be transparent in each face-to-face interview. It's not likely the office will change overnight to accommodate any hyped up expectations a new employee may have.

Attitude

Employers always want employees with the best skills. There is good reason for this. Skills alone, however, do not always translate to a good match for a job or the best employee. While experience can be vital in fulfilling the requirements of some jobs – particularly in the dental office – it can also become a barrier. Jessica may have many years' experience as a dental assistant doing something her way; but if her way cannot be matched up with the doctor's way, there will be disunity and ineffectiveness in the office.

Skills can be trained. Attitude cannot; neither can common sense. One of the most regrettable decisions you will ever make will be the one to hire someone whose attitude or common sense you thought you could change or mold into what you needed it to be.

Finding the employee with the right attitude is like finding a pot of gold coins that fills back up with each and every withdrawal. Consider the following quote by an employee with a great attitude:

> *"My job is in line with the president's*
> *job – to keep people happy."*

Who said that? It was John Wiggins. You don't remember him? John was chosen as the 1995 Ruffies Trash Bags National Sanitation Worker of the Year.[4] Attitude makes all the difference in the world.

Uncle Sam

Dental offices sometimes play loose with the state and federal documentation required for employees. Laws and accepted forms of identification change from time to time. As of this writing, the Small Business Administration cites that U.S. practices have the following responsibilities in order to maintain compliance with state and federal regulations:[5]

- Obtain a signed Form W-4, on or before the start date of the employment.
- Complete Form I-9, Employment Eligibility Verification. Keep I-9 forms on file for three years after the employment date, or for one year after termination of the employee, whichever is later.
- Register with your state's New Hire Reporting Center: A list can be found at:

http://www.sba.gov/content/new-hire-reporting-your-state

Getting the employee who is right for your practice will be one of the best things you have ever done for your business. Keep the government happy with your documentation. Surround your next hiring process with these five keys and you will be on your way to better days. The time to start on the first key is now – before you're in the position of needing to evaluate a hiring decision.

CHAPTER 6

F – Financial Arrangements

Three things keep patients from moving forward with recommended treatment:

- No perceived need
- Fear or anxiety about the treatment, and
- Financial objections

Most every team member can comfortably talk to patients about their need for treatment. It's hard to find a team member who can't be reassuring to patients about the comfort and care of their treatment. Finding those who are willing to talk to patients about the finances related to that treatment is a different matter. Financial arrangements do not need to strike fear into the hearts of team members. What are some guidelines that can help?

People are touchy about their money. Worse still, the only good surprises about money are the surprises that bring the announcement of more of it. Anything that catches people off guard about giving up their money – voluntarily or involuntarily – will be met with closed fists and tight purse strings. Linda Miles says, "To unpleasantly surprise a patient is to lose a patient!" The guidelines below, if followed, take the surprise out of financial arrangements and enable the dental office to help patients past many of the financial barriers they present.

New Patient Welcome Packet

Your New Patient Welcome Packet should contain a copy of your office's financial policies. Include the following information and keep the entire policy to only one page. This page should not be titled, Financial Policies, but rather *Financial Guidelines*. Guidelines or some similar word is less threatening than "policies", especially when it's part of the first communication from the office. The patient needs the information you convey about money matters, so soften the blow and make it as patient-friendly as possible. Cover the following topics in your Financial Guidelines:

- Methods of payment (bank cards accepted, cash, check)
- Guidelines for insurance co-pays and reimbursement, to include PPO plans accepted
- Third-party financing options
- Any courtesy reductions for pre-payment
- When payment is due

- Fees for missed appointments
- Space for the patient to sign and date, indicating acceptance of these guidelines.

You always come out ahead by fully informing patients as to the boundaries of your financial guidelines. Patients come from all kinds of backgrounds and may have had experience with offices that fly by the seat of their pants rather than by anything rational or fiscally responsible. Making sure your new patients know how you run your business will go a long way toward correcting misunderstandings *before* they happen. This eliminates the surprise on the patient's part. It will also help to screen out the few patients who feel they cannot maintain your financial expectations. This eliminates surprise on the office's part. Eliminating financial surprise is worth all the effort you put into it. Communicate your guidelines warmly, and they will be well received by the great majority of patients.

New Patient Interview

When a new patient arrives in your office for his or her initial appointment, it always helps to conduct an informal new patient interview before the patient is seated in the clinical area (see Vol. 2, Chapter 1: N - New Patient Experience). As part of this interview the Patient Care Coordinator or Financial Coordinator will say,

"Mrs. Jones, I see that you have reviewed and signed our financial guidelines, but sometimes patients have questions about money matters which may not have been covered. Do you have any questions for me?"

Mrs. Jones may indeed have questions, and this is an opportunity for you to hear vital information which may help you create the difference between an accepted treatment plan and one that is rejected. You will not be able to make financial arrangements at this time as you do not know what treatment the doctor will recommend. What you *can* do is make sure Mrs. Jones knows you are happy to work with her to minimize the impact of any concerns she may have. And you can be gathering any third-party or other information which her responses indicate may be required for presenting treatment.

Financial Questions in the Clinical Area

Patients often ask the doctor how much their treatment will cost. Doctors serve their patients and practices best when they steer as clear as possible from financial discussions. Providing care and talking money do not mix well. However, there will be patients who will pin you to the wall to answer their financial questions. Avoiding those questions at all costs will come across as a lack of transparency at best, or at worst, deception. When the doctor must answer a question about the cost of treatment, consider the following reply:

> *Mrs. Jones, I understand that you have concerns; I would myself. We're not going to ask you to agree to any treatment without first discussing all the financial issues with you. What I want to do is make sure that you understand the recommendations I am making. Dentistry is my strong point; fees and payments are what Suzanne does best. She is great at helping patients with those matters. You and she will discuss any financial matters before you decide to make an appointment. What do you say to that?"*

Very few patients will object at this point. Taking the conversation in this direction will help you focus on the recommended treatment rather than the money. Once money is introduced into the conversation, it's difficult for the patient to hear or think about anything else.

As a dentist, you should not let Mrs. Jones' request about finances rattle your presentation of treatment. You know what you have found. You know the consequences of doing nothing and the benefits of receiving the treatment. Present your treatment with confidence and Mrs. Jones will have the best opportunity to make an informed decision.

NOTE: Two words that can kill a clinical conversation: money, dollars. Avoid them like the plague with patients in the clinical area.

Selecting a Payment Method

The best scenario results when patients have options to comfortably fit dental treatment into their personal budgets. These options should be developed, as much as possible, exclusive of in-practice payment plans which are both time-consuming and costly to maintain. Cathy Jameson, Ph.D., gathered the conventional wisdom of practice management philosophies and combined it with her own keen insight to pretty much write the book on financial arrangements. Quoting banking research she states,

> "...for every month that an account sits on your own books doing nothing for you...it loses approximately .83% of its worth – a 10% loss during the year. If you have average total collection[s] of $120,000 per year in accounts receivable [with]...approximately 50% of those total accounts sitting on your books at [any] one time...[your annual] loss is $6,000..."[1]

She wisely advises,

"...finance your patients' care without carrying any accounts on your own books...stay out of the banking business. You are a dental practice – not a bank. Do the things that only a dental practice can do and delegate everything else."[2]

When you present treatment to a patient, do so in an incremented fashion that favors the practice. Don't offer patients the easiest method first. For example, if you offer a patient third party financing at zero interest, you could be giving away 10-12% of the treatment cost in fees that you pay to the lender. Cash payment would be in the best interest of the practice. Consider the graduated list of payment methods below, which lists various methods in ascending order of pain to the practice:

- Cash or check (no cost to the practice)
- Debit Cards (1.2-2.0%)
- Credit Cards (2.0-3.5%)
- Third Party Interest Bearing Loans (3.0-7.0%)
- Pre-payment courtesy (5%)
- ACH Debit Plan – (6%)
- Third Party Interest Free Loans (9-13%)

When you make financial arrangements with a patient, the closer you end up to the top of this list, the better. The pain to the practice increases as you go down the list.

On the other hand, the pain to the patient decreases as you go down the list. The best place to meet is where both the practice and the patient are happy. Imagine the following conversation:

Financial Coordinator: *"Suzy, the cost of your treatment will be $4,700. Would you like to pay that in cash?"*

Suzy: *"I don't have that kind of cash".*

F/C: *"Then, you're in luck. We also accept debit cards."*

Suzy: *"If I had the money in the bank, I could just as easily pay cash."*

F/C: *"How about a credit card? Will that work for you, Suzy?"*

Suzy: *"I'm afraid not. They're all maxed out!"*

F/C: *"Then, how about....?"*

You can almost see the Financial Coordinator reaching for Suzy's purse!

Green Acres was a rural television comedy in the '60s. Mr. Haney, the local traveling salesman, came around with his truck loaded down with goods to sell. Anytime a buyer objected to the purchase of any product, Mr. Haney would pull down another rolling shade on the side of his truck to introduce a new offer or a different product. There was no end to the number of offers Mr. Haney had: "If you don't want that, then how about this? Or this? Or this? Etc., etc., etc…"

You don't want your Financial Coordinator to sound like Mr. Haney on *Green Acres*. The best way to avoid or at least minimize this is by gathering clues to financial pain in the New Patient Interview, mentioned above. Suppose Suzy had mentioned to you that she didn't have a lot of cash on hand during the New Patient Interview. Wouldn't it be easier to enter the financial conversation with her as follows, rather than employ Mr. Haney's sell-above-all-else style?

F/C: *"Suzy, you indicated earlier that you didn't have a lot of cash on hand. The treatment you want is 4,700. What were you expecting to pay?"*

Suzy: *"Well, I was prepared for about $1,500."*

F/C: *"So if we can find a way for you to get the remaining 3,200 covered, would that work?"*

Suzy: *"Yes, that's probably what I need to do."*

F/C: *"Suzy, we have a third party who arranges treatment like this to be paid out over time. If they ap-*

prove a payment plan, what kind of payments would work well for your budget?"

Let's stop there. Hopefully, you see that an informed conversation serves you, the patient and the practice much better than just diving in at the top and working your way down a list. It reduces the awkwardness of the conversation. It is more considerate of the patient. And it helps you tailor the financial arrangements in the most beneficial manner for the practice.

If Suzy responded to your last question with $125/month, you might offer her interest free financing to get the remainder paid off over the next 24 months. But if she said, $250/month, you might suggest a low interest-bearing loan or the ACH Debit Plan. While the total cost of either would be about the same, there is less risk to Suzy and minimal risk to the practice. Interest free options carry the risk of high interest (over 20 percent) coming due for the full loan in the event she was late with just the last of 24 payments. Some doctors have the opinion that the financial risk to the patient is the patient's business, not the practice's business. Cartin Coaching encourages practices to do the best thing for the patient, not only clinically, but also financially. Just because a patient can get a loan, doesn't mean that patient can repay the loan. There are moral and ethical concerns for being party to patients overextending themselves financially. Nothing can be gained in the public relations arena from patients who feel they were led down a primrose path, only to hit a financial brick wall.

The benefit to the practice for using a low interest loan or ACH Debit Plan would be that it would recoup at least six percent on the treatment which was financed as opposed to interest-free financing; depending on your choice of ACH Debit vendors, you could recoup as much as eleven percent more than through interest-free financing options. For $3,200 of financed treatment, this could be an additional $352 which the practice would collect.

While working with one practice which was steadily growing, it needed to employ several additional team members over the course of about six months, each in different positions. During the process of three rounds of interviewing candidates, a steady stream of persons either recently or currently employed by a certain "high end" cosmetic practice interviewed with the Office Manager and me. At the beginning of that year this "other" practice had employed forty-one team members. By the end of the year, they had cut back to twenty-three. The word on the street – and voluntarily confirmed by those applicants – was that the practice regularly encouraged senior adult patients to reverse mortgage their homes to finance cosmetic treatment. A changing economy burst the real estate bubble and triggered a chain reaction that burst the practice bubble as well. Preying upon people's vanity or financial ignorance will come back to bite you, as well it should. The Apostle Paul offered wise words when he said,

"The love of money is the root of all kinds of evil."[3]

ACH Debit provider, DocPay™ from Waco, TX, charges the patient a flat fee of $2.50 per month to collect the contracted debt and remit the full payment to the practice.[4] In the final analysis this is the equivalent of having an in-house payment plan without shouldering the responsibility for collecting the money. Patients get extended payment plans without interest; the practice gets more treatment at a lower incremental cost. You will serve your practice and patients well to check into your ACH debit options.

Summary

Some years back, I worked with a dentist whose practice was near one of the most coveted golf courses in the world. When I heard that he was inviting me to play a round, I was ecstatic. He was not my client but had been coached by one of the best. Within a couple holes, he had begun asking me about presenting large treatment cases to patients. He had a $35,000 treatment plan to present the next morning. From hole to hole we talked about the right way to do things and the things to avoid. I confirmed, underscored and encouraged all his coach had taught him. My golf game that day was the pits, but it was fun to watch him get excited about presenting treatment.

The next day when my plane landed back home, I had an email waiting. The dentist had presented the case that morning. The patient accepted and used third-party financing. The dentist and practice were elated and the patient got the full-mouth restoration he wanted. Incidentally, the dentist had never presented a case over $18,000 before this day.

Using sound principles of case presentation will improve the bottom line of your practice. Having confidence in the methods you use will help you close more cases. You'll gain more confidence as you consistently work through these and other methods for helping patients say, "Yes!"

Financial arrangements work best when you stay out of the banking business and find a win-win situation for patients and the practice. Win-wins happens more often when you're able to create a conversation where the financial pain can be informally discovered, such as in the New Patient Interview. Finally, until the patient has been convinced he or she needs the treatment and elects to receive it, there are no financial arrangements which need to be made. When the doctor focuses on the reasons for treatment and the benefits it will bring, the patient is more likely to move forward with appropriate financial agreements. Set your practice up for success by incorporating these principles into your ongoing and daily protocols.

CHAPTER 7

G – Goal-based Scheduling

"Scheduling is the heartbeat of the practice."

—Cathy Jameson

Without a heartbeat, the body dies. Without adequate scheduling systems, the practice withers away; it can also die or, at best, limp along in an incapacitated state for what seems like an eternity. Taking the heartbeat analogy further, your schedule can generate an exceedingly rapid heartbeat that can threaten its overall health. On the other hand, it can degrade to a sluggish heartbeat that provides very little energy for practice growth.

Several years back, my racquetball partner and I were caught up in several long volleys which taxed my heart rate more than I had ever measured – 180 beats per minute. When I visited my primary care physician a few weeks later, I asked, "Doc, is there anything wrong with your heart rate going up to 180?"

Dr. Royal looked at me, startled and said, "What? Why did it get so high? Did you have any chest pain or discomfort?"

"Well, I was playing racquetball and had some long volleys that literally took everything I had. At the next side out I took my pulse and it was 180. I was very tired but I didn't have any chest pain or discomfort."

Dr. Royal replied, "I think you're okay. The problem would be if you couldn't get it up to 180 in a situation like that."

Now, I'm not a cardiologist and neither is Dr. Royal, but what he said made sense to me as it related to my health. It also makes sense to me as it relates to scheduling being the heartbeat of the practice. A truly healthy practice can ramp up to meet the demand for short periods of time without showing danger signs of stress on the doctor, team or patients. Likewise, a cardiovascular system that gets up to the aerobic level of workout on a regular basis will develop a lower heart rate which generally leads to a better quality of life. The parallel applies here, also. Practices that ramp up on occasion to meet high demand or unexpected situations develop an innate ability to handle day-to-day demands without breaking into a sweat. You can have that kind of practice. Developing a healthy cardiovascular system doesn't just happen, and when it does, it doesn't happen overnight. Developing healthy scheduling systems could be the most challenging area of practice management to master. The payoff, however, is more than worth the effort. None of the skills are beyond the reach of dedicated team members at the front desk. They can't do it alone, though; they need the help and cooperation of the entire team. The responsibility for entering appointments into the practice schedule lies at the front desk. But the responsibility for creating an efficient schedule rests with the entire team.

Some years ago working with a client in Cavan, Ireland, I derived one of those great joys from coaching – someone who enthusiastically "got it!" In my previous visit with the practice, we had covered scheduling and implemented some of the basic protocols. We had discussed the scheduling techniques required to make up for time away from the practice when the dentist knew beforehand that he or she would be away (see Vol. 2, Chapter 6: S – Scheduling).[1] A couple weeks after returning to the States, I received a call from the scheduling coordinator in the practice.

Steve," she said, "you know that scheduling technique you taught us that helps to make up for time when the dentist is away?"

"Yes," I replied.

"Well, the dentist is going to The Dawson Academy in Florida for two weeks and staying an extra week for vacation with his family. Do you think we could use that technique to make up for his three weeks away?"

To this day, I'm not sure if her request was a question or a challenge. I responded by saying that I didn't think she could make up *that much* production, but that it would make a great difference to get started right away. The course in Florida was almost three months away. Making a long story short, she was able to give expert attention to the schedule so that instead of losing twelve days of production, she had made up for seven of them before his flight left for Florida. The advanced techniques and treatment presentation skills he learned at The Dawson Academy quickly made up the difference for the other five days and began paying a premium from that day forward!

The techniques described below are variously being employed in many practices on both sides of the Atlantic. What *is not being optimized* is the integration, coordination and intention to combine these scheduling and clinical skills for optimum production and minimum stress. A thoroughgoing detail of the intricacies of goal-based scheduling does not fall within the purview of this short chapter. However, mastering the basic principles of goal-based scheduling can help you achieve better results each day in your practice. Achieving better results by the day increases monthly production and collections. Several basic scheduling concepts must be individually understood, integrated and consistently implemented in the office.

Clinical Delegation

Delegating duties to a clinical assistant is foundational to improving scheduling efficiency in the practice. Each time the dentist legally and ethically delegates a duty he or she could perform to a trained and qualified clinical assistant, the dentist creates an opportunity to do one of two things which help the day's schedule:

- Devote time to other patients/procedures which create revenue while the clinical assistant keeps the revenue flowing in another treatment room. Or,
- Devote time to non-revenue appointments (reviews, adjustments, etc.) so as to reduce the burden of those appointments on the schedule during more productive times.

The first of these results produces more income for the practice. The second result decreases clinical stress in the practice. Since one of the benefits of reducing clinical stress in the practice is carving out more time for premium appointments, the indirect result is increased production as well.

Dentists who are serious about increasing production in their offices will make sure that all clinical assistants have been trained and qualified to do everything that their regulating body allows them to do. When assistants pack cord, make impressions, take radiographs and re-cement temporaries, dentists can see a patient in another room. This generates increased revenue directly or indirectly, simultaneously, in both rooms. The degree to which production can be increased in a practice is directly related to the degree to which clinical assistants are ready to step up to the plate with additional or expanded duties.

Dovetail Scheduling

Like dovetail joints in the four sides of a wooden drawer, a dovetail schedule is one which is interlocked and/or inter-twined so as to have the various parts fit together as a whole. When a dental office schedule is appropriately dovetailed, the dentist can move back and forth from Room 1 to Room 2, back to Room 1, then to Room 3, etc., without undue stress on the dentist or the team. The simplest example of dovetail scheduling is illustrated in the figure, below, for a simple res-toration in Room 1 and an emergency patient in Room 2.

(NOTE: The time intervals in the appointment book, below, have been edited for the purpose of greater detail. You will likely have 10 minute units in your schedule for which this technique works exactly the same.)

Time	Room 1	Room 2
0800	Greet, Injection for MO, # 29	PA (Assistant)
0805	Injection taking effect	Exam (Doctor)
0810	(cont'd)	
0815	(cont'd)	
0840	Next Appointment	

In the simple example above, the doctor greets and injects the patient in Room 1 while the Assistant gets a PA on the emergency patient in Room 2. The doctor immediately slips out of Room 1 while the patient is numbing up and slips into Room 2 to review the PA, examine the patient, prescribe any medications and recommend the treatment which the patient needs. The doctor then slips back into Room 1 before 8:15 to begin the MO restoration on that patient.

This simple example, which you likely already implement in your office, is the basic pattern for more intricate and expanded scheduling protocols. These will enable you to schedule and deliver more dentistry on a given day. It improves upon the scheme of scheduling patients one after the other in a single column or simply staggering them from room to room with no overlap. Your production will increase with each overlap in which your assistant works alone with one patient while you care for another patient in a different room.

If you are not already scheduling this simple example, try it out for one month and see the difference it makes. Block off the first appointment of the morning and the first appointment of the afternoon for appointments which require an injection. By doing so, you automatically create an opportunity for a short appointment in an adjacent room while your first patient is numbing up. It may only take five minutes for a patient to numb up, but it will not endanger the patient or compromise the procedure to give her ten minutes to numb up. What you will gain is the ability to see a second patient for a short paid appointment, such as an emergency. It could also be a non-paying appointment such as a review or an adjustment. Adding these otherwise schedule-killing appointments onto today's schedule in a dove-tail fashion opens up larger, more productive blocks on future days. By optimizing your scheduling protocols in this manner, you increase your capacity for production while reducing stress on yourself and the team.

Opportunities for you to slip out of the room include packing cord, taking impressions, numb up time and others, as well as time for patients to let their jaw muscles relax by gently biting on a cotton roll after long periods with their mouths open. (NOTE: I had questioned the validity of this common advice until a recent long appointment with multiple impressions and extra oral photographs with retractors. When the dentist placed a cotton roll in my mouth and asked me to bite down gently, I was a happy man!) Based on your own philosophy of dentistry, you will be able to significantly improve the efficiency of your scheduling by slipping out of one operatory into another while a well-trained assistant works independently on duties she has been qualified to perform. It will be your responsibility as the dentist to ensure that the assistant is trained to carry out these duties appropriately and to your standard of care or skill.

Blocking Prime Appointments

Three different types of appointments make up your daily schedule: prime appointments, major appointments and basic appointments. The type varies based on the fee which will be due for that particular appointment, not just for an individual procedure.

Type of Appointment	Description
Basic	Unpaid appointment
Major	Paid, but less than your crown fee
Prime	At least your crown fee

The delineation between the various types is a function of the combined fee for the entire appointment. Consider this brief sample fee schedule:

Procedure	Fee	Procedure	Fee
Crown	1,150	Retreat Ant. RCT	900
3-Surf. Post. Comp.	320	1-Surf. Ant. Comp.	175

Now, review the appointments, below:

Appt 1   Crown = 1,150
Appt 2   Retreat Ant. RCT + 1-Surf. Ant. Comp = 1,075
Appt 3   Retr. Ant RCT + 3 Surf Post Comp = 1,220
Appt 4   3Sur Post Comp x3 + 1Sur Ant Comp = 1,135

Given the fee and appointment data above, Appointment #s 1 and 3 are each *prime appointments* because the total fee for the appointment is at least the crown fee (1,150). Appointment #s 2 and 4 are *major appointments* because the total fee paid by the patient for those appointments is less than the practice's crown fee. Any combination of procedures which adds up to the value of a crown fee or above creates a prime appointment when the patient will accept those procedures together for one visit. Quadrant dentistry or even whole arch dentistry provides outstanding opportunities for increasing efficiency in the practice. Longer appointments serve the patient well by helping to reduce stress, reduce the number of injections and reduce the number of times the patient must visit the office to have his or her dentistry completed.

With this background in the three types of appointments, we can take a giant step toward understanding the relationship between appointment type and daily production.

If you consistently schedule 50-70% of your daily goal in prime appointments, you will consistently achieve your daily and monthly production goals.

The implications of goal-based scheduling have more measurable impact on production in your practice than any other single effort you can make.

Consider that the practice whose fees are quoted above works 18 days per month and has a monthly goal of $96,000. The daily goal for the practice would be 5,334. If 25% of this daily goal is hygiene (1,334), that leaves $4,000 as the goal for the doctor each day. In order for the practice to consistently reach its monthly production goal, the doctor will need $2,000-2,800 scheduled each day in prime appointments. Scheduling two crown appointments each day would achieve the lower end of the range. To achieve the higher end of the range, those prime appointments would need to be more valuable appointments or three prime appointments may be required. Some of the factors which will determine the optimum place where your practice falls in this range include:

- the general mix of major and basic appointments seen in your office
- the degree to which hygiene achieves its 25% of the total goal each day
- the degree to which your fee schedule adheres to a given percentile (ie., if your simple restorations were at the 80th percentile for your local market and your crowns were at the 60th percentile, achieving your daily targets may be more difficult)

Working within these scheduling constraints for several months will help you determine where in the range your practice needs to be in order to achieve your daily production goal. This is not an exercise to get wound up tightly about. Some days you will not achieve your goal even with prime appointments scheduled, as desired. Other days you will far exceed your goal. Consistently working the system day by day will yield the results you desire.

Blocking the Production Schedule

Filling your weekly schedule is a lot like filling your personal appointment book: if you don't make room for the big stuff, all the little stuff will take control. Remember the illustration of the glass vase into which a number of golf balls, small pebbles and sand must be fit? In the illustration, there is enough of each of those three items that you can never fit everything in by layering them one on top of the other. The only way to fit everything in is to skillfully combine the pebbles and golf balls while filling in the spaces around them with sand until you get to the top. The only way to build a productive weekly schedule is to weave together major and prime appointments by the day while filling in the remaining schedule opportunity with basic appointments.

Your schedule may currently be full so that you cannot schedule a crown for another seven to ten days. Having your schedule this full will prevent you from being able to move emergency patients quickly into the appointments they need while their pain is still fresh on their minds. The sooner you begin to place the required number of prime blocks on your schedule (50-70% of your daily goal), the sooner you will begin to increase your daily production. Place prime appointment blocks on the schedule for 90 to 120 minutes. You want to block off enough time to deliver a crown *and* a simple restoration or two. If it turns out that all you get to put in the block is a single crown and no additional work, then shorten the schedule block once you put the crown in and create additional room on either side of the block for other patients.

Do not hold the blocks indefinitely. If you have not filled the blocks with prime appointments within two to four days of the unscheduled block, release the block. Fill it with any treatment you can, preferring major treatment over basic. The busyness of your schedule will determine whether you need to release your blocks two, three or four days prior. Prior to being released, only prime appointments should be placed in these blocks.

Business assistants cannot schedule prime treatment out of thin air. In order for them to have options for scheduling prime treatment – and thus, for reaching goals – the practice needs a healthy flow of new patients, effective treatment presentation and appropriate financial options. This combination of healthy systems paves the way for sufficient numbers of patients to move forward with prime treatment.

Effective scheduling is both an art and a science. It requires ongoing attention. The various parameters – length of blocks, when to release, percentage scheduled in prime appointments, etc. – will be an individual practice matter. You will learn to adjust accordingly. As you do, you will see production increase while stress in the practice decreases. This combination creates the kind of practices most dentists dream about but only few achieve. Master goal-based scheduling and the systems which directly support it and you and your team will be at a happier, healthier, more profitable place in the continuing growth of your practice.

CHAPTER 8

H – Hygiene Growth

We expect smoke and mirrors in a magic show, but illusions in the hygiene department can be more like scary *delusions*. Illusions give the impression that things are one way when they are really another. The importance of a healthy hygiene department cannot be overstated. If your hygiene department is growing, your practice is growing. If your hygiene department is in decline, chances are that your practice is also, unless you have supplemented your production with niche or specialty services.

> *If your hygiene department is holding its own, your practice is losing money every day.*

Could this be a contradiction? Let's see why it is not.

This statement, at first, seems at conflict with itself. If the practice grows when hygiene grows and declines when it declines, then why doesn't the practice hold its own when hygiene is holding its own?

Whether it's in the States, the U.K. or Ireland, doctors and team members have an unhealthy tendency to believe the practice is doing well if the hygiene department is holding its own. Nothing could be further from the truth in ninety-five percent of practices. How can you tell if you're among the five percent of practices which can safely disregard this warning? Answer one question:

*Do you have as many patients leaving the practice
each month as you have new patients coming in?*

If the answer is "no", simply holding your own in hygiene is a delusion for both the hygiene department and the operative side of the practice. On the other hand, if the number of new patients you see each month exceeds the number of patients you are losing, your hygiene department is losing ground despite the fact that the schedule may be as full this year as it was last year. How does this work out?

New Patient Growth

For a practice to hold its own in the market, all other things being equal, we generally expect 15 to 25 new patients per month are needed per full time dentist. The low end of this scale would be for established fee-for-service practices with low overhead. The high end would be practices with higher overhead or who are dependent upon PPO contracts. Let's take an example in the middle.

Example

For the past 12 months you have consistently seen 20 new patients per month. This adds up to 240 new patients in the past 12 months. Most doctors agree that 90% of patients should be enrolled in hygiene care at either a routine or advanced level. If we apply this criteria, you're going to need more hygiene appointments for the coming year.

240 NPs x 90% x 2 appt/yr = 432 additional appointments

You can subtract the number of patients you're losing from this total only if those patients were regularly attending hygiene in the first place. Otherwise, if your hygiene appointments are 1 hour each, you will need 54 additional days of hygiene in the coming year.

Wait!

Don't go back to the office and hire a part-time hygienist. You're smart enough to know that adding hygiene days does not mean you are going to deliver more hygiene services. There is probably a reason – or several – why the hygiene schedule has plateaued. Before we look at some common barriers to hygiene department growth, let's unpack what these sample numbers mean.

432 appt x $90/appt = $38,880 in production losses

Chances are, you could absorb many of those 432 appointments into the schedule which is "holding its own".

If the practice is adding more patients than it is losing, the hygiene department will always be growing if it and the practice are healthy.

This is how one doctor for whom I worked grew his practice from scratch to the point of employing four full time hygienists in his solo practice over an eighteen year period. What are some of the barriers which could be getting in the way of the ongoing health and growth of your hygiene department?

Poor reactivation

The time to begin reactivating a hygiene patient who has missed her appointment is when that patient is ten minutes late for the appointment. This should not and does not need to be anything uncomfortable for the patient. Consider the following verbiage from the business assistant at the front desk, Suzy:

Suzy: *"Sally, I'm glad you answered. You're always on time for your appointments and when 2 o'clock passed and you weren't here, I was worried that something may have happened. Are you okay?"*

Sally: *"Yes, Suzy, I'm fine. It's just been one of those days and I absolutely forgot. I am so sorry."*

Suzy: *"Well, you're fine, that's the most important thing. I know you want to stay on track with your hygiene care. When would be a good time for us to get you back on the schedule? You like afternoon appointments and I have two options before the week is out, Wednesday or Thursday."*

Reactivation problems creep up in various ways. Sometimes the office is just busy. Taking care of patients who are in front of us gets priority over those who missed appointments. If you were not able to call Sally at 2:10, perhaps you could have called her at 2:30 or 3:00 or 4:00, but here is a principle to remember:

> The longer you wait to attempt to reactivate a patient who has missed an appointment, the more the patient believes the attempt is about your profit and less about his or her care.

Reactivation calls which are made several months after a missed appointment are almost always perceived as being about the practice and not about the patient, regardless of why you tell the patient you are calling. Attempt to reactivate patients as soon as possible and do so in a way that expresses concern for the patient, not for your schedule.

Many times – consciously or unconsciously – we use new patients to fill the holes created in the hygiene schedule. Existing patients miss appointments and fall through the cracks; new patients take up their spaces for continuous care in the schedule. As a result, the schedule remains filled at about the same level from year to year and the illusion is produced that "we're doing okay". If so, it's not an illusion. It's a *delusion*.

Inadequate Probing Protocol

My colleague, Dianne Watterson, RDH, quotes a study from the *Journal of Periodontology* that showed "...out of 2,448 records chosen at random in 36 dental practices, only 16 percent were complete or adequate in regard to periodontal information." She further relates, "In my chart audits in practices, I have observed a similar situation. In one recent practice, out of 30 adult charts I pulled at random...only two had up-to-date periodontal charting."[1] Taking Dianne's lead, I audited the last 25 patients in hygiene when I visited one of my clients for a consult and found that only three had received a full mouth probing in the past year. Several had no periodontal charting dating back six to eight years. Doctor, do you know what your charts are telling you?

When a new patient is in the chair for a D0150, Comprehensive Oral Exam, the doctor has the best chance he or she will ever have to move the patient into the hygiene schedule. Unfortunately, full mouth probing does not get the attention it should from many dentists and hygienists. Consumers do not sit at home, flip through the television channels and decide to schedule a Comprehensive Oral Exam to relieve their boredom. Something motivated the call for an appointment and the dentist needs to respond to and parlay that motivation into a commitment to ongoing preventive care.

First, the doctor should conduct a full mouth six point probing of each D0150 patient. Before probing, the doctor can say:

> *"Mary, this probe (showing the probe to Mary) is marked with numbers which will tell me how much detachment there is between your teeth and gums. I'm going to place it at six points around every tooth and call out a number that Gina, my assistant, will record. If I call out a 1, 2 or 3, then that area of your gums is normal and healthy. If I call out a 4 or a 5, then we are seeing indicators of the early stages of gum disease. And if the numbers are 6 or above, you will need some level of care beyond a routine hygiene appointment."*

As you call out the numbers, 2-2-1-2-1-5 / 3-5-6-3-6-4, Mary is beginning to diagnose herself according to your protocol and the conversation about hygiene treatment will be more easily engaged.

Weak promotion by the dentist

At the D0150, the dentist should do something which is an exception to the rule, something for which the author is indebted to Cathy Jameson for improving hygiene growth. At the comprehensive oral exam, the dentist should appoint the new patient into the hygiene schedule, if possible. The title "doctor" pulls weight with patients and doctors should use that weight to gently nudge patients into the hygiene schedule. Most treatment rooms have computer screens where the chart or appointment schedule can be pulled up for the doctor and/or patient to see. As the doctor is reviewing his or her findings with the patient, the assistant pulls up the hygiene schedule so the doctor can see the next two or three available appointments. The doctor then says,

DDS: *"Mary, have you ever wondered why dental insurance companies reimburse the full cost of regular hygiene appointments?"*

Mary: *"Since I don't have dental insurance, I guess I never thought about it. But I do have friends who say their insurance covers their hygiene appointment."*

DDS: *"It's really quite simple. Year after year, insurance companies make more money than almost any other industry, year after year."*

Mary: *"Yeah, I've never trusted them a lot, myself."*

DDS: *"The reason for that is that we see them taking our money but they do not like to give it back. They know how to make money. And they know that paying for your preventive care is the best investment they can make to protect their money. By and large, the patients who receive regular preventive care experience fewer major dental problems down the road. The insurance companies invest in preventive care so they don't have to spend so much on what they call basic or major care. If hygiene appointments save them money, you can bet it will save you some as well."*

Mary: *"I never thought of it like that."*

DDS: *"Karen is one of the best hygienists around; her appointment book is usually very full. But she has an opening this coming Thursday afternoon and another one next Tuesday morning. The ladies at the*

*front desk will be working through a list of people who
have been waiting for appointments. Can I reserve one
of these appointments for you before they disappear?"*

The doctor's promotion of the hygienist and her services
goes a long way toward moving new patients into hygiene.
Getting the patient into hygiene as quickly as possible after
the examination sets the stage for quality dental care to occur.
"Calculus, edematous tissue, debris and disease are removed
or controlled. More accurate color matches can be made for
ceramic and composite restorations. And more aesthetically
and hygienically placed margins are made possible. Accurate
impressions minimize hemorrhage and patients are ecstatic
about the treatment outcome."[2]

"Holding your own" in the hygiene department can easily
become smoke and mirrors. If you know what you're looking
at, it's an illusion. If you don't understand what you're seeing, it could be eating away at your practice.

Periodontal probing is a win for both the patient and the
practice. In addition to the patient getting the required care
for his or her condition, the practice improves its production
without any increase in overhead. Ms. Watterson continues,

> *"Another important side benefit of full probing
> on a regular basis is that you will discover
> more periodontal disease. Non-surgical treat-
> ment of periodontal disease is the most produc-
> tive procedure a hygienist performs. So, it*

follows that your production will increase as you detect periodontal disease and schedule treatment. You cannot treat it until it is diagnosed, and periodontal probing is the way it is detected."[3]

A Hygiene Check-up

Check your charts; check your numbers. Pull the charts of hygiene patients seen over the past two or three days and make a note of where your practice currently stands. If your probing protocol is not where you want it, ask your hygienist to review the charts also. Schedule fifteen or twenty minutes to meet with her to develop an action plan which will help you deliver better care to patients and increase the profitability of your practice.

Stay on top of hygiene as the bread and butter of your general dentistry practice.

- Reactivate
- Educate
- Probe
- Appoint new patients right away

You'll stay ahead of the hygiene challenge. If that's not enough, you will notice that the restorative side of the office benefits from the referrals which are generated as you and your hygienist work together to grow the practice.

CHAPTER 9

I – Initial New Patient Phone Call

*"You never have a second chance
to make a first impression"*
—Anonymous

Your new patient experience begins the moment the phone rings with a prospective patient on the other end of the line. Here is your chance for the practice to shine above any others the patient may call. Do your job well. Even if the patient phones other practices, he or she will likely come back to you based on the overall quality of the call and the information you shared. Cartin Coaching trains the Initial New Patient Phone Call with timeless principles of business, sales and customer service, all bundled within our *Six Steps for Appointing New Patients.* It will be good to both hear the conversation *and* note the principles which come into play. Let's get started.

Greeting

Answering a business phone professionally and warmly involves four key elements:

- a greeting,
- identification of the number reached,
- the name of the person the caller is speaking with, and
- an extending of one's hand

"Good morning. Clearview Family Dental.
This is Fran. How may I help you?"

A bright, cheerful greeting always speaks well for a service which people love to hate. Very few people admit they enjoy going to the dentist or hygienist. Setting their minds at ease from the start is a great way to move closer to a booked appointment.

What about "cute" greetings?

I once made a cold call by phone to a prospective dentist client and was greeted by, "Good morning, Camden Family Dental. This is Amy; how can I make you smile?" Amy's voice was so enthusiastic and cheerful that she absolutely disarmed me from the start. What made this work for her when other business assistants shutter at the thought of answering their phone in that manner? The clear answer is that Amy was genuinely excited to engage a new caller to the practice. Cute can come across as fake. Professional can come across as stale. With Amy, it came across wonderfully because the first principle for answering phones is to be genuine. Business assistants who dislike greeting, getting acquainted with and problem solving with new people will be as unhappy at the reception desk as the dentist who secretly dreams he was a test pilot. In addition to the greeting, the new patient call also includes five other key elements.

Connecting

The business assistant should get the name of the caller when she responds to the caller's answer to the question, "How can I help you?"

Fran: *"Good morning. Clearview Family Dental. This is Fran. How may I help you?"*

Caller: *"I'm looking for a dentist and wanted to find out what it would cost to get an appointment in your practice."*

Fran: *"Well that's wonderful. Thank you for calling. Whom do I have the pleasure of speaking with?"*

Caller: *"My name is Greta Garvin."*

Fran: *"I'm pleased to meet you by phone, Greta. How did you hear about our practice?"*

Greta: *"My friend Sherry Glass is a patient of Dr. Finkel's. She said I should check with you guys before making a decision."*

Fran: *"That is so sweet of Sherry. We love having her in the office. And she's right – Dr. Finkel is an exceptional dentist with a reputation for some of the finest work in Georgia. I want to give you an accurate quote so I need to know more about what you need. What led you to call about an appointment with Dr. Finkel today?"*

In about forty-five seconds, Fran has greeted Greta, connected with her and brought referral magic into the conversation by discovering Sherry's trust in Dr. Finkel and team. Fran will want to use Greta's name in the ensuing conversation about two or three more times, depending on the length of the call. People like to hear their names. More than that, repeating it a time or two helps the business assistant to get it right as well.

The best answered calls are those where the caller perceives that he or she has the total attention of the person at the other end of the line. Patients can "hear" you typing even when no sound escapes from the keyboard into the phone. There are those undeniable pauses such as getting an address correctly entered – "three…fiiiii…fteen Marrrrr..shall Street, right?" – pauses which signal that the caller, is trying to get information, what is really happening is that someone on the other end of the line is filling out a form about her. Remember, most people do not enjoy visiting the dentist. If for this reason only, business assistants should make every effort to make the call as pleasant as possible. It is recommended that a pre-printed New Patient Call-In Form be used for taking down data during an initial call (see Appendix). While you can't enter an appointment in your software without getting patient details entered first, you can always go back and complete the details after the call. Extend the patient the honor of being heard and understood before introducing the drudgery of being profiled and recorded.

> *Extend the patient the honor of being heard and understood before introducing the drudgery of being profiled and recorded.*

Once you have a commitment for an appointment, then you can switch to computer entry by saying,

"Greta, let me get a couple of your contact details into our appointment system to reserve your time."

At this point, the caller understands that you need the information and obtaining it becomes a more courteous and friendly endeavor. After all, until the patient has stated that he or she would like to have an appointment, there is no need for obtaining anything other than the patient's name and the referral source (in this case, Sherry Glass).

Once the business assistant makes a connection with the prospective patient, it is time to move to the next phase of the call.

Exploring

Patients call for one of three reasons. Knowing the reason for their various calls will help you to respond to them in the best possible manner. Patients want to see a dentist because:

- They are motivated by something positive (new in town, finally have insurance coverage, realize it's about time, etc.
- They are not totally satisfied with their current dentist.
- They are in pain.

The sooner you discover the particular reason for this call, the sooner you will move toward a booked appointment rather than wearing the caller's patience thin.

For example, if the reason for the call is that the patient is in excruciating pain, you don't have to build value for the appointment – he already understands the value: getting out of pain! What this patient is looking for is a quick appointment that will address his pain and put him on the road to a speedy recovery. Likewise, if a patient is shopping around for a dentist because she's new in town and wants the best care possible, she would rather hear about the latest technology, gentle injections and three consecutive "Dentist of the Year" awards. She's probably not greatly interested in whether she can get an appointment the very next day. The conversation Fran began with new patient, Greta Garvin, continues with some explanatory notes to follow:

Fran: *"Why are you looking for a dentist at this time?"*

Greta: *"Well, I moved here about three weeks ago and met Sherry at the Junior League. When I mentioned all the frustrating things about moving to a new town, the dentist naturally came up. Sherry thinks very highly of your office, I thought it would be a good idea to go ahead and contact you, just in case. I saw my dentist maybe five or six months ago so there's no real hurry."*

Fran: *"It's great that you called, Greta; I want to help you get established with a dentist. Our new patient assessment provides a comprehensive look at your complete oral health. It sounds to me like it would be the best way for you to get started here in Clearview. May I tell you what this includes and give you the fee for that assessment?"*

In the script above, Fran has determined which of the three motivations has driven Greta to search for a dentist in Clearview. Now she can put her best foot forward in meeting the exact need Greta has. Once the reason for the appointment has been determined, it's time to move to a phase of the call where Clearview Family Dental can really shine!

Building

This is Fran's opportunity to set Clearview Family Dental apart from any other dentist in town. She has opportunity to build value for the appointment before quoting the fee. Picking back up the conversation...

Fran: *"May I tell you what this includes and give you the fee for the assessment?"*

Greta: *"Yes, that would be great."*

Fran: *"Thanks. Your appointment will actually begin with our patient care coordinator, Suzanne. She will go over your medical history and any concerns you have so that she can make sure you get the best care possible. Dr. Finkel's assistant will get some photos of your teeth and smile, externally with a camera and from inside the mouth with small intra-oral camera. Then after x-rays, Dr. Finkel will meet you and begin a tooth-by-tooth review of your mouth, checking for any decay, any excess mobility, signs of excessive wear; and he will evaluate your bite and any issues related to TMJ. He will also perform an oral cancer screening. Finally, Dr. Finkel will gently probe six points around each tooth to assess the* *health of your gums and determine what level of hygiene care you will need. I know that sounds like a lot and it is – Dr. Finkel is very thorough. We have some of the latest technology to insure your comfort; although you won't need any injection for this visit, patients remark all the time about how gentle Dr. Finkel is. Your appointment will take about an hour and fifteen minutes and the fee for all of this is just 189. Depending on any dental insurance you may have, you portion could be a less or even at no cost to you.*

My New Patient Appointment Experience

Several years back when I relocated to a different area, I phoned 12 practices in my new hometown, asking the same questions of each practice as I looked for a new dentist. As a consultant, I was eager to see how this "initial new patient phone call" would be received and managed on the part of each practice. None of these practices knew me or knew any connection I had to dentistry or practice management coaching. In addition to the normal questions, I added one that I thought surely someone would bite into:

"What kind of further education has your dentist had since graduating dental school?"

Four results of that "survey" were eye-opening. Here are the specifics:

1)   All of the practices were within $10-20 of each other for comparable services.

2)   No one tried to "sell" me on the benefits of visiting their practice.

3)   No one recommended that I review their website or any online patient reviews.

4)   When asked about further training after dental school, the identical answer from each practice (in their own words) was, "He/she goes to all the CE courses."

Why, after being prompted, did these business assistants not see this as an opportunity to brag on their doctors? What made this answer more interesting was that a number of the practices had websites which listed various postgraduate training the doctors had undertaken – Pankey, Dawson, LVI, AGD, etc. As we say here in the South, these business assistants should have jumped on that question like a duck on a june bug! They didn't.

In the end, the only thing that remained as a discriminator between one practice or the other was price. Personally, I didn't want the cheapest price but many patients will. I reviewed the websites and online information again and made my decision. I also decided in the future to help dental teams identify some crucial elements of these "first impression" calls to their own offices. Teams need ample training in how to sell their doctor and practice to the patients who phone in for information about appointments.

Do you want a majority of patients taking up your "loss leader" comprehensive oral exam because it's the lowest price they could find? How far will that go when you recommend anything beyond a simple restoration? How eager will those patients be to move forward for several quadrants of much-needed scaling and root planing? The best position to be in with new patients is having new patients in your chair who have chosen you not based on price, not based on insurance alone but based on the educated opinion that you offer the best quality and value of any practice in town.

Building value for the new patient exam in your practice should be an easy sell. This isn't hard core selling. It's soft selling – telling the prospective patient why your practice is a great choice for the concerns they have. Once this "selling" portion of the call is completed, it's time for the business end of the conversation. Many practices lag behind their potential because business assistants are reluctant to take this next important step. It's the one step in the process that, more than any other, can actually *put* a new patient appointment on the books.

Closing

"You have not because you ask not." Without applying any pressure, the business assistant should make an attempt to schedule the patient for an appointment. The net should be drawn in a friendly, inviting manner. Two great Zig Ziglar quotes come to mind about *closing the sale.*

> *For every sale you miss because you're too enthusiastic, you will miss a hundred because you're not enthusiastic enough.*
>
> *Timid salesmen have skinny kids.*

Greta: *"189? That sounds like a lot. I was going to ask about the hygiene appointment, it sounds like this doesn't include a cleaning and I wanted to get that on the same day. I have ZebraLife Insurance and I saw that you were listed in my book."*

Fran: *"Wonderful – that will help you and we are happy to file your insurance for you if you'd like. About the hygiene -- many of our patients feel the same way. The doctor needs to do a hygiene assessment before he can prescribe the level of hygiene care you need. What we've found, also, is that the occasional patient who gets both in one visit feels it's a bit much for one day. You'll get outstanding, comfortable care* *this way. We'll be fully informed on your dental needs and able to provide you the very best care possible. Can I reserve an hour on Dr. Finkel's schedule for you, Greta?"*

Greta: *"Yes, that will work."*

Fran has worked through the new patient scheduling protocol in a masterful way. She negotiated her way around the always tricky ground of bringing patients in through hygiene. Fran gently affirmed the patient's insurance plan and summarized why making the appointment was the best decision for Greta. Finally, she asked the closing question and she made it clear in a courteous way that the schedule belongs to the doctor, not to Fran. Bringing the authority of the doctor's name and reserving *his* time on the schedule helps guard against the patient thinking that a cancellation will only affect Fran's appointment book.

Following Up

Every new patient deserves a follow up before the actual appointment day arrives. Your follow up should be two-pronged, consisting of a New Patient Welcome Packet and a confirmation call. Generally, you want to confirm the patient a couple days in advance. Remember that you have no history with this patient and cannot assume he or she will show up. The New Patient Welcome Packet will be covered in more detail in Chapter 1 of Volume 2: N – New Patient Experience. Your follow up to the initial phone call serves as the bridge between this first telephone impression and the first impression your new patient will experience on the day of the appointment. Make the bridge between these two shores of contact and more patients will cross over to become loyal members of your patient family.

Every practice differs. The verbal skills your business assistant uses need to be matched to the protocols you have implemented in your practice. For example, you may bring in new patients as a D0150, Comprehensive Oral Exam. Or you may bring them in through the hygiene department. Having an experienced third party evaluate your new patient protocols will often highlight portions of the new patient experience which you have mastered but are not showcasing to their full potential. Value-building communication and further refinements can be integrated by an expert coach or consultant to help you put your best foot forward in the New Patient Experience. As you refine the verbal skills for your Initial New Patient Phone Call, carefully evaluate the entire New Patient Experience so you can build on that momentum. Consider also the value of obtaining a qualified, unbiased review of your new patient protocols....because *you never have a second chance to make a first impression.*

CHAPTER 10

J – Job Performance

"I thought I wanted a career;
what I really wanted was a paycheck."
—Bumper Sticker spotted in Augusta, GA

NOTE: The system of job performance accountability that is described below was derived and modified from the author's experience in the U.S. Air Force and has been adapted and used with excellent results in non-profit, small business and dental practice applications.

Is the car in the above quote parked in your staff parking area? Let's hope not. Getting your employees to perform up to the standard expectations of the job can be a difficult job in and of its self. Leading a team is not for the faint of heart. Dental practice owners can find themselves in situations where they have one standout performer, one piece of dead wood and everything in between. Dentists must sometimes feel like the Prophet Ezekiel of the Hebrew Scriptures. In the sixth century B.C., the Prophet Ezekiel heard from God through a vision in a valley full of dry bones (Ezekiel 37:1-4):

God: "Ezekiel, can these dry bones live?"

Ezekiel: "God, only you know."

Do you ever wonder if some employees will ever come to life? The dentist may fret and fume over the performance of a staff member. While owning a business has never been guaranteed to be an easy job, it doesn't have to be this hard. The complicating factor in the dental office is the inescapable reality that the "boss" must sit in one chair for six to seven hours each day with his or her hands in the mouths of customers needing exact, expert and immediate attention. Where is time to help staff members more fully execute their daily duties in an acceptable manner?

Achieving satisfactory performance from employees begins with the hiring processes and decisions covered in Chapter 5, E – Employing Staff. Team members should always have an up-to-date and accurate job description before accepting any offer of employment. Anything less invites the opportunity for failure at worst, disappointment at best. Let's begin with the...

Job Description

Potential employers should ALWAYS have a reliable job description to present to a candidate for any position (This book doesn't employ "all capital letters" often). The time to begin achieving better job performance from your staff is *before* you hire them. This is not to say that corrections can't be made mid-stream. Often, the best of circumstances have come about simply because corrections have been made *along the way*.

Cartin Coaching's in-practice training opportunities include a session with the entire team in which job descriptions are refined and updated as needed. Doing this by fiat from the dentist's private office will not achieve the best results. We recommend updating job descriptions through a team exercise where the opportunity for discussion and input creates ownership and buy-in. Here's how to take a first step toward improving the job descriptions in your office:

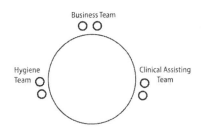

Consider the team meeting being conducted in the adjacent diagram. The dentist is not shown in the drawing but serves as the facilitator for the meeting. For the sake of simplicity in explaining this exercise, the practice is made up of two business assistants, two clinical assistants and two hygienists. These functional groups provide valuable input into the exercise and, by doing so, help to identify areas of confusion which need to be cleared up. Dr. Dentist leads the team through a step-by-step process to improve the accuracy and completeness of all job descriptions in the office.

Step 1: Distribute one sheet of paper to each functional group of team members – business team, hygiene team and clinical assisting team. Ask each team to write the title of their functional role at the top of the page: business assistant, hygienist or clinical assistant.

Step 2: Ask each functional team to list all the duties they are performing in the practice. Each functional team is to work among themselves to:

- List all the duties which are currently performed by members of that functional area.
- List these duties whether or not they are on their current job descriptions.

Example

The business assistants routinely sterilize instruments, even though it is not part of their job description. They believe this is the responsibility of the clinical assistants. Regardless, the business assistants list it on the job description worksheet for their functional area.

This exercise will be more productive if you ask each functional team to go to a separate area of the practice where they will have privacy to discuss and work on their own functional area job description. Allow 15 minutes.

Step 3: Gather the teams back together around the table or room, remaining in their functional groups. Have each group to pass their draft job description clockwise to the next group.

Step 4: Ask each group to work on the job description they just received by adding any duties to the list that they think the previous functional group has omitted.

Example

The clinical assistants are printing tomorrow's schedule each afternoon to use in preparing for the morning huddle. They have just been passed the job description for the business team. Thus, they add this duty to the business team's job description worksheet because they feel it is a better fit since the only printer is at the front desk.

Allow 10 minutes and again let each functional team go to a private area to work together.

Step 5: Gather the teams back together around the table or room, remaining in their functional areas again. Pass the job descriptions again so that each functional team now has a job description in front of them that they have not yet worked on. Give the same instructions as in Step 4. Allow 10 minutes, again allowing each functional team to work in a private area.

Step 6: Gather the team back together. Dr. Dentist now takes up the job description worksheet from each functional team. She lets them know that she will review each description to add anything which may not yet be listed and to move around items she feels should be the primary responsibility of other functional teams. You can conduct this exercise regardless of the number of team members you have or even if there is only one team member in any particular functional area.

Step 7: Update the job descriptions with the additions, deletions and edits you believe to be appropriate and make a copy for to keep for yourself. Give each team member a copy of your version of the updated description for their functional area several days before the next team meeting. You will want to edit some job descriptions to be different from others in a particular functional area. For example, the Office Manager's job description may contain much of what is on the business assistant's description. However, there will be additional duties on the Office Manager's job description which are not on the one for the business assistant and vice versa: At the bottom of each job description, add one additional duty:

Update this job description on the back of this sheet by adding duties which you may be performing daily, weekly, monthly, quarterly or annually – whether those duties are performed voluntarily or per the direction of a supervisor/team leader.

Step 8: At the team meeting, discuss each job description and help the team to understand your decisions, where possible.

Step 9: Formalize the job descriptions by having each one typed and formatted in a presentable manner.

Step 10: Give each team member a copy of their updated job description to sign and date. Dr. Dentist keeps a copy of each signed job description and lets each team member retain a copy for him or herself.

NOTE: It would be prudent to check with an HR expert from your state or state dental association to ensure you understand any implications from updating a job description for an existing employee in your state without any further formal action. Employment laws vary from state to state; regulations governing what any dental team member may or may not do also vary from state to state.

Substandard Performance

No one wants to be the bearer of bad news. However, just because you have a good job description doesn't mean employees will adhere to that job description in a satisfactory manner. Also, just because an employee has a state or national certification doesn't mean he or she will perform duties satisfactorily either. It is important in a dental office that an employee not only do a job right but also do it the way the dentist wants it done.

These matters and more can land dentists between a rock and a hard place with employees more often than not. How do you deal with an employee who is not performing his or her duties satisfactorily? Even if your state is a "right to hire" (which really means "right to fire") state, you do not wish to upset the apple cart in the office or in the life of an employee whom you need to terminate. Dentists often struggle along unhappily with a team member's performance, wanting to make a change but feeling deep down that something more should have been done before now or something different should be done at this time.

"Some people – no matter how much you give them or how much you try to help them improve their performance...are not going to change. At least not now, and not as a result of anything you are doing. Accept it, and it will get easier to take the necessary steps to make an ending."[1]

Terminating an employee is a costly decision (see Chapter 5: E – Employing Staff). It will most likely affect the morale of the team. Patients will notice the turnover. The decision to terminate an employee should be the final option. What is the doctor to do?

Documentation

Now that you have good job descriptions for each role in the practice, a training plan is a simple next step. Simply take each duty from the job description and enter it into a spreadsheet with nine columns, portrayed in the series of figures below.

Column 1	Column 2	Column 3	Column 4	Column 5
	TRAINING			
	TRAINER		TRAINEE	
Job Task	Initials	Date	Initials	Date
Duty # 1				
Duty # 2				

A qualified trainer should be identified to train each item on the Training Documentation Form. Training should be accomplished in the following manner:

1) The trainer demonstrates the task.

2) The trainee performs the task.

3) The trainer certifies that the trainee can do the task.

4) The trainee initials and dates, indicating confidence that he or she can perform the task proficiently.

You should allow time between steps 3 and 4, above, so that the trainee can practice the task several times to ensure he or she can repeatedly perform the task correctly. Answering the phone correctly could be completely signed off in a morning or afternoon. Packing cord correctly may take a week or two to sign off. Don't fret that you don't have everyone signed off on every task immediately. The important thing is that you are making forward progress and achieving a level of job performance accountability which you have previously been unable to achieve.

Column 1	Column 6	Column 7	Column 8	Column 9
	RE-TRAINING			
	TRAINER		TRAINEE	
Job Task	Initials	Date	Initials	Date
Duty # 1				
Duty # 2				

Once an employee has been signed off on a task, it is his or her responsibility to continue performing the task at a satis-factory level. If performance slips, notice that the last four columns on the sample form have been provided for re-training.

Notice that the two tables on pp. 117-118 will actually comprise one spreadsheet with nine columns total. The contents of each of the nine columns are:

- Column 1 – Task to be trained
- Column 2 – Initials of the trainer
- Column 3 – Date training was completed
- Column 4 – Initials of the trainee
- Column 5 – Date trainee signed off proficient
- Column 6 – Initials of trainer for re-training
- Column 7 – Date retraining was completed
- Column 8 – Initials of trainee for re-training
- Column 9 - Date of renewed proficiency

Retraining is accomplished in the same manner as training. One exception could be that you allow the employee more time between steps 3 and 4 to ensure he or she is fully up to speed before signing off on the retraining section. Signing off on the retraining section of the Training Documentation Form should make an impression on the employee that job performance has been documented and trained and now has been retrained and documented. The Training Documentation Form should be kept in the employee's personnel record. Should the employee become a burden to the practice due to repeated poor job performance on one or more key tasks in the practice, the data will be readily at hand to make the case for further intervention or, if necessary, dismissal.

The goal is not to create a system which makes it easy to terminate employment. The goal is to create an employee accountability system which:

- Clearly spells out expectations
- Provides adequate training for all tasks to be accomplished
- Takes into consideration the need for occasional retraining
- Provides the documentation needed for cases of habitual under-performance that can be used in administering discipline or addressing salary or bonus issues
- Provides the documentation needed for cases of habitual under-performance that is needed to make the decision to terminate a staff member's employment.

Creating a good system for job performance accountability can never eliminate all the pain that accompanies troublesome personnel decisions, but it can take the sting out of those difficult decisions. It will also leave you with a clear conscience that, as an employer, you went the extra mile to develop the employee into a successful team member.

CHAPTER 11

K – Knowledge Base

*"Knowledge has to be improved, challenged
and increased constantly, or it vanishes."*
—Peter Drucker

Where does your team stack up on the knowledge curve? If Peter Drucker is right (and he's not usually wrong), what are you doing to improve your knowledge? What are you doing to challenge it? Is the knowledge base in your practice being increased constantly? The term knowledge base covers a lot of ground. It covers those things that are new or emerging in the field of dentistry as well as those that have been around for some time and become "standard" in the industry. When we say knowledge base, we are also talking about each member of your practice. Likewise, we do not confine the term to clinical topics alone. The title, *Practice Management from A-Z: A Readable Guide to a Healthy Practice* reflects our position that to manage your dental practice well, you need to execute practice management systems which embrace these topics and more. To the topics covered in Volume 1 and 2 of this book, you need to add team topics, business topics, marketing topics, clinical topics, even life topics. How can you parlay a growing knowledge base in your practice into a healthier practice for you, your team and your patients? This is a good point for us to consider the bottom line, but not just any bottom line.

.

The Triple Bottom Line

Every business owner understands the term bottom line. Understanding the Triple Bottom Line will take you further down the road of success. Ken Blanchard says,

> In high performing organizations, everyone's energy is focused on not just one bottom line but three bottom lines – being the ***provider of choice, the employer of choice, and the investment of choice.***[1]

When you become the *provider of choice*, systems for attracting and retaining patients really begin to hum. The community – consumers and healthcare referrers – know your reputation, trust it and have confidence in securing or recommending your services. Imagine what that does to supercharge your marketing budget. As you become the *employer of choice*, attracting and retaining the brightest and best team members makes you the envy of practices throughout your market. The savings in hiring and training costs alone will make a significant impact on your future retirement portfolio. Rather than sorting through scores of mundane applications and résumés, you consult a file of star talent to determine which three you wish to bring in for an interview. And being the employer of choice pays off in dividends which can't be directly deposited into a bank account. Happier, more congenial team members and a less stressful practice define the offices where the entire team is exactly where they want to be and fulfilled in the roles they carry out on a daily basis. Finally, you want to be the *investment of choice.* Dr. William F. "Bill" Davis, an experienced transition consultant, often reminds dentists of a sober fact:

Someday, every practice will transition.

When it does, what will its financial pay-off be? How much will it command on the market for dentists who are looking for a practice to purchase? What will a younger dentist find its value to be when he or she is looking to buy in as a partner? How much will it pay out to your spouse when an untimely death catches your family off guard? The quality of your practice will determine how much others are willing to invest in it during a time of transition. But being the investment of choice is not just for the inevitable transition down the road. It also applies to the value of your practice today when you are applying to a lender for a loan for any number of practical reasons. Integrating Peter Drucker's words into what we've learned, if the knowledge in your practice is not being improved, challenged or constantly being increased, here's what you can expect:

- Your reputation as the provider of choice is slipping.
- Your position as the employer of choice is giving way to someone else.
- Your ability to borrow or sell your practice for what you think it is worth is diminishing.

If, on the other hand, your knowledge base is being improved, is being challenged and is increasing on an ongoing basis, you're on the way to bankrolling your Triple Bottom Line into the stuff that entrepreneurial dreams are made of. Your fluency in a growing knowledge base improves all your bottom lines. And your knowledge base must be examined according to several criteria.

Modernity

By the end of World War II knowledge was doubling every 25 years. Today things are not as simple as different types of knowledge have different rates of growth. For example, nanotechnology knowledge is doubling every two years and clinical knowledge every 18 months. But on average human knowledge is doubling every 13 months. According to IBM, the build out of the "internet of things" will lead to the dou-bling of knowledge every 12 hours.[2]

For many dentists this means not only the need to stay ahead of the curve but to look around and see where the pace of change may have left you behind. Are you resisting elec-tronic charting or still filing insurance claims by hand? Are you logging onto various payer websites picking off outdated benefit information for patients and dependents or using a cutting edge service such as Insurance Answers Plus? Are you coding with confidence or having claims denied because of outdated codes and insufficient documentation? You un-derstand measuring an individual's IQ, intelligence quotient; we recommend an assessment of your KQ, knowledge quo-tient, as well, which will assess your practice along a continu-um of modernity and other factors discussed in this chapter.

Dentists typically stay better informed about ad-vancements in clinical dentistry than about business or admin-istrative concerns. There is a price to pay for falling behind in either. Recently, Cartin Coaching conducted an Insurance Analysis of a general dental practice in a western state. The business assistant who filed insurance claims was new to the dental industry and had worked in the practice for just over three years. She received only two weeks of training from the lady who retired. Her lack of knowledge and the former team member's inattention to detail had created a loss leader situa-tion out of what should have been a bread and butter proce-dure. Under the major PPO in the practice, the office was charging $48 less for a procedure than the fee schedule allowance of $85 – a loss of 56% of what the payer had agreed by contract to pay. This real world example demonstrates what Peter Drucker terms challenging your knowledge base. Having an outside expert to review the key facets of your practice can bring matters to light which would have otherwise been hidden losses in the dark.

One area where the knowledge base has markedly changed over the past few years is the area of human resources. A steady stream of changes continues across the country and varies from state to state. For example, one practice in the Southwest found that a hygienist with a four year degree is subject to the rules and guidelines for an exempt worker (*ie.*, manager, no overtime) while the same team member with a two year degree had to be paid overtime. These discoveries do not usually occur in the day-to-day operation of the practice but can be readily pointed out by legal counsel in the event of a dispute or termination hearing. For a variety of reasons, it's easy to see why dentists need to give careful attention to the changing knowledge base which dental offices are subject to in a rapidly changing landscape in the industry.

Proficiency

An earlier chapter referred to a quote which stated,

Wisdom comes from experience;
experience comes from mistakes.

While this principle holds true across all aspects of a practice, you cannot afford for it to figure into the wisdom with which you deliver dentistry to your patients. Clinical mistakes can be very costly, both to patients and to the practice. Your knowledge base plays a crucial role. Constantly improving your knowledge base with procedures, protocols and pharmaceuticals allows you to deliver the very best dentistry in the safest manner.

Based on the type of practice you have, the rates you pay for malpractice insurance can vary by thousands of dollars per year depending on the number of hours of continuing education that you have completed. When an insurance company gives a subscriber a break, it's time to sit up and take notice. A discount on malpractice insurance rates which results from higher levels of continuing education courses is the insurance industry's way of quantifying an important reality:

Your knowledge base can reduce the risk
to patients and, thereby, decrease the likelihood
that your practice will be threatened due to an
oversight in accepted standards of care.

The more proficient you become as a dentist by increasing your knowledge base of both clinical dentistry and administrative matters, the more successful you will be at reaching your goals. This applies to firing same-day crowns in your office (technical/clinical). It also applies to filing the appropriate supporting documentation and/or narrative for payment submission which would otherwise be turned down by an out-of-network provider (administrative/financial). How are you staying on top of the ever-increasing base of knowledge in the dental world today? Is your progress in this area limited mostly to clinical concerns? What could be identified in your practice by way of clinical, financial, marketing or administrative processes which may be either costing you money or putting your practice at risk?

Team Member Skills

Consider two situations:

Situation 1:
You and each team member have good skills.

Situation 2:
You and each team member excel in your respective roles and crafts.

The difference between the two defines your competitive edge. Jim Collins reminds us in his book by a similar title, "Good is the enemy of great."[3] The ability of team members to carry out supportive tasks with great ease enhances the value they bring to the practice while decreasing stress on a daily basis. Take a look at the following two team members, Suzy and Geri.

Suzy and Geri job share as business assistants on the front desk. Suzy works Monday and Tuesday. Geri works Wednesday and Thursday. They enjoy their part-time roles and five days off each week. Suzy has worked as a business assistant for three years and has mastered the practice management software. So has Geri, although she has only been in the job for 16 months. Suzy jumps on rejected claims immediately and always has them resubmitted within two days. Geri does also. At the end of every work day, charts have been properly filed by each lady and the next day's charts have been pulled and provided to the dental assistants and hygienist. Everything that Geri does, Suzy does equally well...except one thing. Suzy struggles to use word processing, spreadsheet and slide presentation software while Geri works through these auxiliary tasks with comfort and ease. The only difference between these two business assistants is their proficiency with office productivity software. If you assign each of them equal portions of practice management software reports, electronic claims submission, chart filing, recall postcard generating and spreadsheet work, who is going to have time left over to work on the practice rather than just working in it?

The illustration does not suggest that you should let Suzy go. Rather, it implies that Suzy needs to increase her knowledge base and that by doing so she will be more valuable to the practice. What if you had two Geri's? Aside from their unique personalities and temperaments, it is possible. One hour each week dedicated to online tutorials in spreadsheets could pay for itself in a month and begin paying dividends for the remainder of Suzy's time in your employment. The more you and your team members invest in improving the knowledge base throughout the practice – in primary roles and in supportive functions – the more your practice moves from good toward great.

Another possibility is that your team members are implementing the systems you have in place to their fullest capabilities but you are not achieving the level of results which are to be expected. In this case, it is no lack of effort on the part of team members that hampers production and collections in the practice. Often it is the systems which need to be enhanced or modified to allow for continued growth. Cartin Coaching & Management organizes its proprietary practice growth methods around *Seven Systems for Success*:

- Strategic Systems
- Communications Systems
- Team Building Systems
- Marketing Systems
- Business Systems
- Clinical Systems
- Treatment Acceptance Systems

As a complimentary exercise to reviewing this book, you and each of your team members may navigate to the following link to compile a foundational analysis of the *Seven Systems of Success* in your practice in less than 10 minutes per team member:

http://www.cartincoaching.com/evaluation.asp

Whether it is specific skills which need to be improved or systems needing refinement, the degree to which you address those needs will determine the rate at which you begin your climb to the next level of success. The same principles hold true for the dentist; however, the payoff soars exponentially higher when applied to the chief producer of revenue in the practice. For this reason we need to consider it under a heading all its own.

Marketability

If you refer out endo, adult ortho and implants, you are fulfilling your potential to the practice no better than Suzy who only wishes she had the option of referring word processing, spreadsheets and slide presentations to Geri. The more dentistry you can deliver as an expert in your own practice, the sooner you will achieve an all-around expert status which Dr. Bill Williams of Suwanee Dental Care (GA) calls *Decathalon Dentistry*. Like all other major undertakings, making this transition one step at a time and sticking to your plan will help you to pace yourself and achieve your goals without burnout. An action plan to get started can be as simple as follows:

Step 1: List all the dentistry you are currently referring out.

Step 2: Rank each service by interest level with "1" beside the service which excites the most passion within you, "2" beside the next most appealing service, etc.

Step 3: Rank each service by an honest appraisal of what you could do best, with "1" beside the service which is the most natural fit for your clinical, intellectual and hands-on abilities, "2" beside the next best fit, etc.

Step 4: Rank each service by the level of economic promise it offers for the practice, with "1" being most profitable, "2" being next, etc. In this evaluation consider such data as:

- the fee you could reasonably charge for the service
- the degree to which the service would be covered by the major dental insurance plans in your market area, whether or not you accept assignment of benefits
- how many other providers in your market area are actively providing and marketing the same service
- the ongoing cost of providing the service (incremental costs)

Step 5: Beside each service, total the three numbers you assigned to that service in your ranking process

Step 6: Like golf, lower scores are preferred. The service with the lowest total score represents your best opportunity. Going for the best opportunities first creates more revenue to drive your economic engine. It will also instill added confidence in your ability to develop into a *Decathalon Dentist*. As you get to the more difficult items on the list, you will have expanded skill, confidence and knowledge levels that make each step feel less threatening and more achievable.

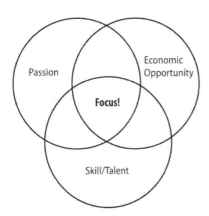

Working through the above exercise employs what Jim Collins calls the *Hedgehog Principle*, adapted in the figure to the right. It is that principle which combines your passions, skills and the economic drivers to identify the area of focus which will generate the greatest dividends for your effort.

For the next five years, commit to adding two new services which you will provide at a high level of expertise. Encourage and empower your team members to increase their skills accordingly. Guide them to strengthen the supportive skills needed in their respective roles. Your practice will be at a very different level. You will be energized by the lower stress and higher profit that live at the intersection of passion and skill. Your practice will be less of what frustrates you on a daily or weekly basis and more of what it *can* be as you grow toward the future.

What's next for your team?

What's next for you?

CHAPTER 12

L – Leading Your Team

There are two types of leaders;
those who do and those who don't.
—Steve Cartin

L eading a dental team from chairside challenges the best of dentists. How does an owning dentist provide leadership throughout the office while he or she is busy at the hands-on work of dentistry six to seven hours each day? It starts with...

Trust

Definition: Leadership is influence.

Actions speak louder than words. Too often, the actions of the leader replace *influence* in this short definition with efforts to *control, pressure, demand or drive*. While all these words create something akin to influence, only trust creates high and healthy levels of influence among those you lead. Underline this next statement and commit it to your ongoing thinking:

Others will submit to your leadership even if they don't trust you, but only so long as it suits their personal agenda.

Just because someone is following your leadership today, doesn't mean they trust you or that they will follow you to-morrow. Where little or no trust exists, something "not good" is going to happen when your agenda and the agenda of those you're leading collide.

Dentists may try to overcome the mistrust of a team by buttering up individuals, paying them higher salaries, contin-ually reminding them of the great dentistry being done or charitable dentistry provided for the poor, etc. Once trust has been destroyed, rebuilding it is a long and difficult matter.

Trust may be considered a soft skill but if it is, it is a soft skill that brings lasting results. The trust that individual team members have in you binds them together into a formidable force for success, customer service and a happier workplace. As David Horsager says in his excellent book, *The Trust Edge*, "Trust is not simply a dish in your leadership buffet. It is the table holding up the smorgasbord of talent demonstrat-ed by your team every day."[1]

"One of the reasons a redwood forest is so strong is that the roots not only spread deep

but also spread wide. They connect and inter-weave together to form an even stronger net-work of roots. It is the same with trust. We are our own trees but are strengthened enormously by being connected with others [through trust]. "[2]

Leading vs. Managing

Popular arguments arise over who is to be preferred – a leader or a manager? The best resolution to that question is to see leadership and management as two sides of the same coin. If we were applying this chapter to a multinational corporation – Xerox or Exxon-Mobil – it would be easier to see the leader as someone who involves himself in relatively little hands-on management at the lowest levels of the organization. In a small business and particularly in a dental practice it is virtually impossible to untangle management from leadership. The dentist drives revenue for the practice with the work of her hands as she works closely with other members of the team. This highly relational work environment between the leader and the team melds together the complementary roles of leadership and management. The dentist who handles these roles well will be leading even while managing and managing even while leading. The typical arguments for leaders vs. managers are better suited for academia than the local dental practice. My retired Navy dentist friend and businessman, Dr. Robert Loar reminds us,

> *"Leadership is six months down the road in time; management is today. Management ensures cooperation and commitment to the team goals by small course corrections and esprit de corps; leadership, by studying depth charts and current charts and deciding on a destination."*[4]

Cartin Coaching & Management ascribes to the leadership and management theories within the framework of servant leadership espoused by scholars like Robert Greenleaf, Ken Blanchard and John Maxwell.

Rather than seeing leadership and management as qualitatively different functions, consider that the leader must function well in two roles: 1) the vision/direction role, and 2) the implementation/management role. The traditional organizational structure with the leader at the top communicates the vision/direction role well. The team expects the leader to provide these functions. Individuals sometimes want to do jobs the way they want to do them; but, when it comes to the broader direction of a business, these same people do not want to be at the desk where the buck stops. As a leader, you provide a vision/direction role that only you can provide. You are responsible for providing the vision/direction for the practice.

"The most pathetic person in the world
is someone who has sight but no vision."
—Helen Keller

The vision you provide can be for the day, the week, the month, the year or even the long-term vision/mission. It can be for the patient about to be seated in the treatment room. While you as the practice owner are responsible for vision, they – the team – must be *responsive* to you and to the vision which you have established for the practice; they must buy into your vision.

Once vision/direction has been established, it is now time to turn it all upside down. In the ongoing implementation phase, the team is largely responsible for carrying out the vision. As the leader, *you must now become responsive*. Now it is your role to make them successful in all reasonable ways. You are to remove obstacles, provide resources, ensure training, etc. – all so that individuals and the team can be successful in carrying out your vision. Likewise, you do well to become the biggest cheerleader, spurring them on to bigger and better successes in the days ahead. The leader must guard against overemphasizing the "everyone-answers-to-me" atmosphere which is so prevalent in many offices. Such an atmosphere smothers creativity and clobbers customer service.

My wife, Sandra – a vegetarian, called a local pizza parlor to order pizza that I was to go pick up. I overheard the conversation as she asked what the special of the night was –

two medium five-topping pizzas for $20. Not a bad deal. Her end of the conversation went like this:

> *"I need one medium thin crust pepperoni, green peppers and onions. And I need another thin crust with green peppers and onions. And the third and fourth toppings I want are more green peppers and onions."*
>
> [Pizza parlor now talking]
>
> Sandra: *"But I just want four toppings and you said it included five-toppings."*

From what I heard, I figured that it could not be any two of the same toppings; I interrupted, "Don't worry, Honey, I'll take care of it when I pick them up." So I thought.

The young lady met me at the counter. It was the beginning of the evening rush hour. She opened the boxes, showed me my two pizzas and then presented me with the bill for $22 -- $2 extra from the peppers and onions.

"My wife only wanted four toppings total. The two repeated toppings weren't expensive items like cheese or meat, just peppers and onions."

"I'm sorry, that's our policy," she said. "It has to be five different toppings."

I couldn't give up. I just couldn't bring myself to do that.

"Could I speak to a manager?"

At this point, the young lady walked back to the counter where a middle-aged lady was spreading sauce over crusts. She looked up at me, somewhat in disgust it appeared. The evening rush crowd was gathering behind me; we all heard her loud, impatient voice: "Tell him I don't have time to talk to him; I'm busy making pizzas!"

The young lady came back to the counter and started, "She said..."

"That's okay," I interrupted, raising my hands in a "giving up" gesture, "I understand completely."

The local pizza parlor lost a long-time customer over a $2 quibble about policy. The point here is that the young lady was doing exactly what the manager wanted her to do – she was prioritizing service to the boss over service to the customer. Whenever a leader demands the hierarchical position as the team implements the vision, that leader forces the team to serve him or her rather than the customer (patients). But when team members are allowed to serve the customer within the framework of the vision, it creates a win-win-win: practice, team and patients.

This is not the inmates running the prison or the tail wagging the dog. While serving the vision, the team must accept responsibility for their decisions. It is what we call self-directed leadership. When leaders force their team to adhere rigidly to every jot and tittle of a policy or come to them for routine decisions, they stifle creativity, growth and customer satisfaction. Blanchard says that if the leader empowers the team during the implementation phase, it creates the opportunity for the team to…

Soar like eagles.

When the leader remains at the top as someone to whom all must give obeisance, it destines the team to…

Quack like ducks.

Typical duck phrases include:

- It's not my job to _____. (fill in the blank)
- I just work here.
- Put it in the suggestion box.
- That's our policy.

Self-directed Team Members

This chapter is titled Leading Your Team. Leading your team requires that the team is moving in the same direction you are moving. Team members don't get to redefine the mission, values or overarching business systems which make up the practice. Every time a team member makes and carries out a decision rather than coming to you for approval or for a decision, it frees you to stay focused on the work you have in front of you. Every time a team member *can't* or *won't* make a decision he or she *could* make, it creates an interruption, robs you of time and complicates the task on which you are focusing.

The production in your practice is not directly proportional to the number of team members you have. It *is* directly proportional to the number of self-directed leaders in your practice. So a large part of leading your team is actually developing the leaders around you. Just as an assistant "leads" in the operatory by taking an impression or packing cord, so also you need front desk assistants who lead by making decisions within your boundaries. For example, a business assistant leads by making a decision concerning a copay amount that was quoted in error and a hygienist leads by making a decision about the voice-activated system which isn't working for her probing.

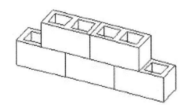

Each time you create another self-directed leader, you add a block to the foundation for growth. The wider the foundation, the higher the profit can reach. On this stack of three foundation blocks (self-directed leaders), three additional blocks (profit) can be stacked. But if you add one more block (self-directed leader)

to the bottom, *six* other "profit" blocks can rest upon the foundation. The bonus side effect to developing leaders around you is that as you do, the demands on the ongoing HR systems in the practice begin to decrease. Creating a self-directed team doesn't just happen but the effort you put into it will pay off in increased dividends on an ongoing basis every day you open the door for business.

Leading Change

The words coach and consultant are used almost inter-changeably in the practice management arena. But these words are not synonyms. They each describe a different pro-cess and desired outcome. Consultants dispense information – good information, but dispensing information does not re-sult in changed behaviors. As a dentist who dispenses valua-ble information to team members and patients on a daily basis, you know this firsthand. If those who received that in-formation implemented it correctly and maintained proficien-cy carrying it out, it would only be a matter of weeks before you had the practice of your dreams. Consultants can't build a practice by their presence and/or content alone. The prac-tice must have self-directed leaders to facilitate positive change. If communicating valuable content does not produce change, where can we turn for help? This is where Cartin Coaching takes off the consultant's hat and put on the coach's cap. Consider the difference between a consultant who communicates valuable information and a coach.

The word *coach* goes back to pre-Victorian England in the days when horses pulled carriages around London to get passengers from one place to another. The word for carriage, a private vehicle, evolved into coach – a vehicle for hire. Even today in England, the word coach is used for vehicles "hired" from one spot to another while bus is reserved for public transport on a prescribed, recurring route. As time passed, this word has morphed into many uses with the same connotation. Consider the following: baseball coach, workout coach, life coach, vocal coach and even practice management coach. In each situation, the "coach" has the purpose of helping the learner (baseball player, singer, hygienist, etc.) to improve his or her performance through careful attention to instruction, practice, evaluation and careful observation of the person's strengths and passions. The derivation of the word and its original meaning need to be kick-started back into practical usage:

> *A coach takes people from where they are to where they want to be. Coaching assumes the willingness of the passenger to trust the driver, pay the fare and remain for the entire journey.*

The Process of Leading Change

Thus far we have examined the topics of trust, leading vs. managing and self-directed team members. Now we turn to the important consideration of leading change. First the leader must nurture and develop trusting relationships with the team. Another early part of the process is for the leader to decide if he or she will "step down" from lofty authoritarianism and serve the team by removing obstacles, providing resources, training and encouragement. The goal of all his hard work is to develop self-directed team members and this can only happen as the practice owner leads change. This final section on Leading Your Team describes the process of leading change from two crucial but different aspects.

External Change

By external change, we are talking about a change in behavior. Something needs to be happening that is not happening at the present time. You want to lead the front desk to respond more positively to price shoppers or your assistant to consistently pack everything required in the baggie that goes to the lab. Behavioral change also includes key decision-making skills that facilitate other external actions. An example of this could be that the hygienist with the malfunctioning voice-activated system remembers that this has happened three times in the past month, makes a decision and follows through with the decision to call the IT vendor. When it comes to external change, an ongoing process is required to take a person from "beginner" to "master" in any endeavor of work or life.

Beginner

The Beginner doesn't know what she doesn't know, like the first time many of us got behind the steering wheel of a manual transmission vehicle. Beginners are high on commitment and low on competence. Beginner enthusiasm is expressed in such phrases as, "I don't know why everyone in town doesn't come here for their dentistry," or "This is the most amazing team I've ever had a chance to work with." The beginner needs a trainer who will focus on instruction and oversight. He or she should be given little, if any, room for decision-making. The beginner should be closely supervised even when working alone. The beginner needs a supervisor/trainer.

Learner

Beginners advance to become learners. At this stage, the competence is still fairly low and the enthusiasm has waned. This is the point where employees transition from saying, "This is the best practice in town," to saying, "If I had known all this, I'm not sure I would have taken this job." Most employees who don't make the cut are lost either at this level or because of poor conflict resolution skills at higher levels. While the beginner should receive instruction and oversight from a trainer, it is a coach that the learner needs. This is why true coaching is such hard work. The one being coached needs to get past certain roadblocks – usually a combination of handling confrontation and receiving correction and training. The learner must deal with all this while keeping his or her attitude in check. The learner stage is complicated by the fact that the learner may not have foreseen any of these challenges when applying for a job in your practice. Unlike the beginner behind the wheel of the manual transmission vehicle, *the learner now knows what she doesn't know.* In so knowing, she is cautious not to take on a task which is beyond her capabilities. Problems of ego, insecurity or an oppressive work environment often lead to the learner coming up short in his or her ability to perform the key functions of the role which is assigned.

Achiever

Organized unions speak in terms of apprentices and journeymen. The terms apprentice and journeyman correspond, respectively, to learner and achiever in Cartin Coaching's workplace assessment. The worker who has transitioned to the achiever stage is one who is fairly committed and highly competent. The achiever gets behind the wheel of the same car and *knows what she knows.* She has achieved a high level of skill. She certainly does not need instruction and oversight. Neither does she need practice and evaluation. So the achiever doesn't need a trainer. She doesn't need a coach. What the achiever needs is a consultant. The consultant brings resources, experience and support to introduce additional skills or fine-tune skills which are already in place.

You need seventy percent or more of your team to be at the achiever level or above to have a healthy, happy practice.

Master/Trainer

The person who has reached the level of Master/Trainer gets behind the wheel of that same vehicle and drives home from work during rush hour, stopping on hills, downshifting after a sudden near miss and easing through congested traffic. The surprising thing is that she doesn't even remember changing gears from the time she left the office until she pulled into her garage: *She doesn't know what she knows.* Her skills have become second nature and she is capable of completing tasks without thinking about them, the same tasks which made her tremble in fear just two or three years earlier. Consultants and coaches are beneficial to master/trainers primarily in specific new tasks or protocols which the master/trainer wants to add to his toolkit. However, the primary need of the master/trainer is for a mentor, someone who has walked the road which the master/trainer is walking. The mentor is someone who inspires the passion of the master/trainer. Perhaps you notice that the master is also a "trainer" and, thus, in a perfect position to begin working with a novice. As you develop master/trainers in your practice, you can delegate much of the ongoing work of training your team to these committed leaders. Developing team members to the master/trainer level forgoes the need to hire outside trainers, coaches or consultants, except where new protocols are being introduced to the office or it's determined that a third party would be best for the practice. External change is part of the process of leading change. Real change has a further dimension.

Internal Change

Real change is complicated by the fact that the facilitator or practice owner cannot make it happen. There is a compartment of it to which only the trainee or team member has the key that unlocks the door of possibility. Like external change, Cartin Coaching sees internal change as a four step process.

Knowledge

One's knowledge base is the easiest thing to change. You bring in a speaker, share a book, attend a conference, watch a video, sit in on a webinar. The list goes on and on. Some of the growth which needs to happen in your office will require new knowledge to be introduced.

Attitude

Whoa! Change someone's attitude? You're correct; none of us can change someone's attitude. It can only by changed by the person who owns it. This is why a poor attitude should be the single most disqualifying factor when hiring a new employee. Let's take smoking cigarettes as an example. You can give someone the knowledge that smoking causes cancer, increases the risk of heart disease, etc., but only that person can decide he or she wants to stop smoking. The same is true with an employee who needs to adopt different behavior. You can give her the knowledge as to why the behavior needs to change and how to implement that change, but only she can decide if she wants to change.

Behavior

Wanting to stop smoking and stopping it are two different things according to those who have developed the habit. While not chemically-driven, work habits are also engrained and are only changed through diligent attention and commitment. This is why, in Chapter 10 – J: Job Performance, we noted that inacceptable performance should be nipped in the bud with correction and retraining rather than allowed to continue unchecked.

Organizational Change

If leading individuals through change is difficult, leading an entire team through change is more difficult still. A team is comprised of individuals who must depend on each other, trust each other, support each other and cover for each other from time to time. Not everyone accepts change at the same pace. Guiding the organization (practice) through the change process takes patience more than pressure.

Understanding the four steps of internal change will help you to make critical decisions which will affect the development of your team and practice. It bears repeating: One of the most critical aspects of any employee's relationship with your practice is that person's attitude about their work, their fellow team members and the practice owner. You can hire trainers, coaches, consultants and even mentors. Team members must want to receive the knowledge, have an attitude of openness to change, commit to the daily implementation of new ideas and work hard as a team to change the organization. These concepts have been incorporated into Cartin Coaching's assessment processes for helping practices develop customized team training plans. You can enable your practice to grow by careful attention to these principles as well. Work on them patiently but consistently and watch your practice begin to improve.

Dipping back into the previous chapter, let's touch on Knowledge Base once again as it relates to leadership. John Maxwell says,

> "If you want to lead, you must learn. If you want to continue to lead, you must continue to learn."[5]

Continuous learning is prerequisite to continuous leading; further, you must implement, evaluate, refine and establish by habit and demonstration, not by decree or policy.

Now you're ready for your next cycle of learning and leading.

CHAPTER 13

M – Morning Meetings

A properly executed morning huddle
can increase your production by 10%."
—Cathy Jameson

Morning meetings/huddles give you an opportunity to line up your day, iron out last-minute wrinkles and identify opportunities for increased production. Teams who have not been conducting a morning meeting often object that such a meeting will take too much time. Your morning huddle should take no more than 10 minutes. Experience has confirmed time and again that in 20-30 minutes of coaching the team, teams with multiple dentists and multiple hygienists can conduct their own morning huddle in just 8-10 minutes.

If you see your first patient at 7:30 am, you can have your meeting at 7:15, be out by 7:25 and have a few minutes to catch your breath before calling the first patient back. The secret to an efficient morning meeting is everyone knowing his or her part in the meeting and arriving prepared to make the contribution which has been assigned to them. The Office Manager or Business Team Leader should conduct the morning meeting. If two such persons work in the office, rotate it a week at a time to keep the energy and focus more fresh. Each team member should have been provided a copy of the day's schedule which was printed at the end of the day yesterday. They will use these to make notes on patients in preparation for the meeting and to add any pertinent notes which come up in the discussion. With a marked up schedule in their jacket pockets, team members can take a quick look at what's coming up at any time and place in their day.

As all meetings, begin the morning huddle with something positive. This is a good time to acknowledge an extra effort by a team member the day before or to ask about the local primary school parent's night which you may be aware that some of your team members attended. Keep it personal; there's plenty of time for the business coming up. The order below is a good option both for the progression of the meeting and the material to be covered. Consider the script under each heading to get a feel for how the meeting might progress.

Positive Opener

Ofc Mgr: *"Good morning, everyone. Has everyone seen Jessica's Facebook photos of the dance recital last night? Go* *ahead, Jessica... do a little boasting. From what I saw, it's well-deserved."*

[Jessica shares some things and the team joins in mom's excitement]

Ofc Mgr Continues: *"A great night was had by all. Let's get a good day started."*

Production/Collections Update

Ofc Mgr Continues: *"As of yesterday, we're $2,300 behind our production target for the month. We have four days left to work and we can work together and make that up. We're ahead in collections by $3,100 but that's due to the large case with Mrs. Stodlemeyer which came through on Care Credit, about $9,600. Carrie is working hard to get some of the A/R in the door so if she's seems busier on the phone that usual the next few days, that's probably why.*

We'll make up some of the production today if the schedule holds; we've scheduled $800 above our daily goal."

Prime Appointment Blocks

Ofc Mgr Continues: *"Doctor's next prime appointment block is this coming Wednesday, the 29th at 10:00 but there's some flexibility to move it thirty minutes either way. And the* *next prime block in hygiene is on Marci's schedule, Tuesday the 29th at 2:00."*

[NOTE: A prime appointment on the operative side is any appointment for which the total production for the procedures delivered in that appointment equals the practice crown fee or above. A prime hygiene appointment equals the fee for a quadrant of scaling and root planing. Knowing the availability of the next prime appointment on either side of the schedule helps the doctors, assistants and hygienists to be alert for opportunities on the day to move patients who need prime treatment into those appointment blocks (See Chapter 7: G – Goal-based Scheduling).]

Emergencies

Ofc Mgr Continues: *"We don't have any emergency appointments scheduled yet today but the phone was ringing off the hook when we stepped into the meeting, so let's make sure we're prepared. Doctor, what's the best time for you to see an emergency patient today, other than our 2 o'clock block?"*

Doc: *"First, thanks to Kim for staying late yesterday to help me see the guys from the basketball team at City College. It's good to give back to the community and I couldn't have done it by myself. Job well done. I need to call the accountant this morning and I think I can be out of the room with Mr.*

Watson at 11:30, so if we have a second emergency, tell them we can seat them around 11:45 and I should be able to see them shortly after. "

Ofc Mgr: *"Now let's move to the operative patients. Kim, you go first this morning. "*

Dental Assistant Review

Kim: *"Jessica will be finishing up when the doctor steps out to make his call at 11:30 so I'll get the overflow room ready for the emergency if one gets booked. Mrs. Smith at 2:20 called back twice about her new denture so we've got her in today. John Carter at 9:30 is overdue for radiographs so let's try to get him seated a little early if he's here and I think I can get him to have those done. That's it for me; how about you, Jessica?"*

Jessica: *"Mrs. White at 3 o'clock is trying to get her work done before her granddaughter's wedding in a couple months. Remember to say something about that to her. And Sharon Wood is coming back in to get her last crown. She's been really happy with the whitening and restorations thus far, so I think she'll be a good opportunity for a referral. I'll see if I can do that and will let you know at the front desk if I had the opportunity or not. That's it."*

Ofc Mgr: *"How about hygiene, Marci?"*

Hygiene Review

Marci: *"My day is full unless someone cancels. Jimmy Barton needs a quad of SRP so I'll see if I can get him in that prime block next Tuesday. I have two patients who are overdue with radiographs and I'll see what I can do with them. Jackie?"*

Jackie: *"Geri Ann Sanders will be in at 11. Her teenage twins haven't been in in over a year. I know she has insurance so I'm going to work on getting them booked. My first four patients today need probing so, Kim or Jessica, if either of you would be available for a couple of those, that would help me stay on schedule. I'm through."*

New Patients

Ofc Mgr: *"We have a new private pay patient this morning. Doctor, you're seeing Greta Garvin at 9:30. She's excited because Sherry Glass referred her. So remember to mention Sherry. [Turning to the doctor]...What do you have for us?"*

Doctor's Time

Doc: *"I just need to make sure that someone calls Dr. Eades' office about the case I sent over for him to review. The patient is coming in again tomorrow and I'd like to hear from him before then, if possible. Remember, he's an hour behind us but if someone gets a message to him, I'm sure he'll call me back this evening. Oh, we need to get the IT folks in to see what's happening to the images when I try to move them between monitors in Operatory 3. Janice, will you call them and let me know when they can come?"*

Ofc Mgr (Janice): *"Sure will. Our service contract says they will respond within 3 days to a non-critical service issue. I called them last Friday and will check back with them today."*

Closing Positive Note

Ofc Mgr Continues: We've got a pretty full schedule and Carrie is making a lot of calls on the A/R. It's going to be a busy day. Let's be mindful of each other today and stay on top of our A game. Remember, you may be the one to make the difference whether someone has a good day or a bad day. Be the best YOU that you can be.

Reading through the sample Morning Huddle script, you notice that your meeting should:

- Begin and end on a positive note
- Keep production and collection numbers appropriately in the team's mind
- Identify the next prime appointments on both the restorative and hygiene side
- Plan for added emergencies which may come up
- Review opportunities for added production, radiographs, recall appointments on the operative and hygiene side
- Identify patients who are good candidates from which to obtain a referral
- Cover issues of concern to the dentist

The morning huddle covers matters of interest to that day's schedule and patients. A good huddle is both friendly and informal. Chit chat should be kept to a minimum and saved, if time permits, for after the close of the meeting. A good morning huddle can help you increase production on the day, identify opportunities for added production in the weeks ahead and even generate referrals from Raving Fan patients like Sherry Glass. Team members come in a few minutes early to work off of the printed schedules, reviewing patient records on paper charts or in the computer. The better plan is to have them review the charts the afternoon before.

With just 10 minutes or less invested together in a morning huddle, you can deliver more exceptional care to patients, increase practice production and decrease stress in the office.

You're going to like your new morning huddle!

Afterword

"Success in life is founded upon attention to the small things, rather than to the large things."
—Booker T. Washington

"I don't look for seven-foot bars to jump over; I look around for one-foot bars I can step over."
—Warren Buffett

Y ou can do this! The two men quoted above believe you can do this. I believe you can do this. The first of these men became very rich inside by tending to the things around him which he *could change*. As a result, many others became rich inside and became financially successful as well. The second man charges $1 million for someone to have lunch with him and then gives the money to the poor. When he speaks, the economy of the world listens. He achieved his success by stepping over one-foot bars, not by hurdling over towers.

Practice Management isn't rocket science. I have known too many very successful dentists who have never had a coach or consultant in their offices. By and large these were men and women who did things correctly from the very start. Old habits are hard to break; sometimes they are also hard to admit.

These thirteen chapters are here for your benefit, to help you take a fresh look at some one-foot things. Yes, there are a couple two-foot things here and there, but everything is within your reach. We're happy to help by phone or in person should you desire a third party assessment and guidance. This is most helpful when you have resistant team members or have created ruts in your practice by doing things in less than ideal ways for too long. It is also a great plan when some aspect of your knowledge base needs to be strengthened.

Tend to the small things in this short volume and you will have a much happier, much healthier practice. And watch for Volume 2, N through Z, which is planned for publication by early Fall, 2014. If you identify with the philosophy of dentistry we espouse at Cartin Coaching & Management, you will want to check out and, hopefully, recommend the books on the following page as they become available:

Last year, at the *Emerging Leaders in Dentistry Conference* hosted by the Christian Medical & Dental Associations, Dr. Peter Dawson shared the secret of his success.

A note card.

A three-by-five note card upon which he would write down small things he wanted to implement. He tucked the card into his shirt pocket at the beginning of each day and worked on the small things. Then, he checked each one off upon completion. Doing the small things worked out very well for Dr. Dawson. It will work out well for you, too.

Booker T. Washington, Warren Buffett and Dr. Peter Dawson – that's pretty good company.

Join that company by doing the small things and, as Zig Ziglar was fond of saying, "We'll see you at the top!"

Practice Management from A to Z: March 2014
A Readable Guide to a Healthy Practice, Vol. 1

Coming Soon

Dentistry by the Book: July 2014
Integrating Life, Work and Faith
Co-written with Dianne Watterson, RDH and
featuring a bonus chapter with Dr. Jeff Amstutz

Practice Management from A to Z: September 2014
A Readable Guide to a Healthy Practice, Vol. 2

Practice Management from A to Z, October 2014
UK Version in One Volume

Endnotes

Opening Quote

1. Henry Cloud, Necessary Endings (New York, NY: Harper Books, HarperCollins Publishers, 2010), 90.

Chapter 1

1. http://www.businesswire.com/news/home/20130812005275/en/Merchant-Cash-Capital-Releases-Study-Two-Thirds-Small#.UyDKsPldXTd (dated August 12, 2013).

Chapter 2

1. Max Lucado, Cure for the Common Life (Nashville, TN: Thomas Nelson, Inc., 2005), 1, 140.

2. Ken Blanchard & Phil Hodges, Lead Like Jesus (Nashville, TN: Thomas Nelson, Inc., 2005), 5.

3. http://www.aoa.gov/Aging_Statistics/ (accessed February 13, 2014).

4. Federal Interagency Forum on Aging-Related Statistics. Older Americans 2012:

5. Older Americans, 2012: Key Indicators of Well-Being. (Washington, DC: U.S. Government Printing Office, 2012), 24.

6.   Tom Rath, Strength Finders 2.0 (New York, NY: Gallup Press, 2007).

Chapter 4

1.   Dr. Gary DeWood, http://www.dentistryiq.com/articles/2013/03/11-ideas-for-leading-your-team-in-the-dental-office.html (accessed February 8, 2014).

Chapter 5

1.   Gayle Smart, ed., Powerful Practice, Vol. 1 (Roswell, GA: James & Brookfield Publishers, 2006), 167.

2.   http://www.sba.gov/community/blogs/facebook-credit-checks-criminal-records-where-law-stands-employee-background-checks (dated July 12, 2012).

3.   Henry Cloud, Ibid., 96-97.

4.   Kevin W. McCarthy, The On-Purpose Business (Colorado Springs: CO, Pinion Press, 1998), 37.

5.   http://www.sba.gov/content/10-steps-hiring-your-first-employee (accessed January 30, 2014)

Chapter 6

1.   Cathy Jameson, Collect What You Produce (Tulsa, OK: PennWell Corporation, 2005), 59.

2.   Ibid., 22.

3.   Cited from 1 Timothy 6.10 (Scripture taken from the New King James Version. © 1979, 1980 and 1982 by Thomas Nelson, Inc. Used by permission. All rights reserved.)

4.   Note: In 2006, after GE purchased Care Credit, all of Care Credit's former DirectPay business (ACH debit) was turned over and incorporated into DocPay's business and business processes.

Chapter 7

1.   Steve Cartin, Practice Management from A to Z: A Readable Guide to a Healthy Practice, Vol. 2 is due for release early Fall, 2014.

Chapter 8

1.   Dianne Glasscoe Watterson, The Consummate Dental Hygienist (Frederick, MD: Professional Dental Management, Inc., 2011), 57.

2.   Interview with Dr. Robertson Loar, February 24, 2014.

3.   Dianne Glasscoe Watterson, Ibid., 59.

Chapter 10

1.   Henry Cloud, Ibid., 49-50.

Chapter 11

1.   Ken Blanchard, et. al., Leading at a Higher Level (Upper Saddle River, NJ: Blanchard Management Corporation, 2010), 4.

2.   David Russell Shilling on www.industrytap.com, dated April 13, 2013.

3. Jim Collins, Good to Great (New York, NY: Harper-Collins Publishers, 2001).

Chapter 12

1. David Horsager, The Trust Edge (New York, NY: Simon & Schuster, 2009), 12.

2. Ibid., 37.

3. The author is deeply indebted to the thinking and writing of Ken Blanchard for the material which follows in this chapter, integrated from the following sources *Leading at a Higher Level* (*ibid.*) and *Like Jesus* (*ibid.*).

4. Interview with Dr. Robertson Loar, February 24, 2014.

5. John Maxwell, *Leadership Gold* (Nashville, TN: Thomas Nelson Publishers, 2008), 126.

Appendix

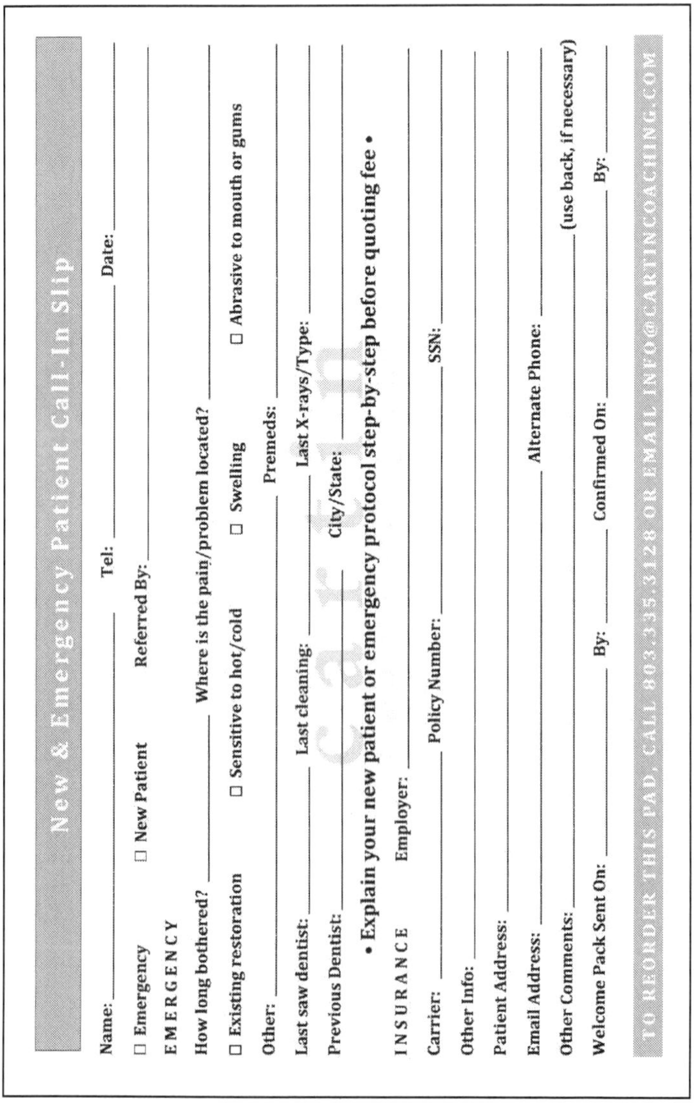

New & Emergency Patient Call-In Slip

Name: ______ Tel: ______ Date: ______

☐ Emergency ☐ New Patient Referred By: ______

EMERGENCY

How long bothered? ______ Where is the pain/problem located? ______

☐ Existing restoration ☐ Sensitive to hot/cold ☐ Swelling ☐ Abrasive to mouth or gums

Other: ______ Premeds: ______

Last saw dentist: ______ Last cleaning: ______ Last X-rays/Type: ______

Previous Dentist: ______ City/State: ______

• Explain your new patient or emergency protocol step-by-step before quoting fee •

INSURANCE Employer: ______

Carrier: ______ Policy Number: ______ SSN: ______

Other Info: ______

Patient Address: ______

Email Address: ______ Alternate Phone: ______

Other Comments: ______ (use back, if necessary)

Welcome Pack Sent On: ______ By: ______ Confirmed On: ______ By: ______

TO REORDER THIS PAD, CALL 803.335.3128 OR EMAIL INFO@CARTINCOACHING.COM

Made in the USA
Charleston, SC
22 May 2014